| File | | Edit | | Formula | |
|---|---|---|---|---|---|
| New... | | Undo Clear Ctrl+Z | | Paste Function... | |
| Open... | Ctrl+F12 | Repeat Clear | | Define Name... | |
| Close | | Cut | Ctrl+X | Create Names... | |
| Links... | | Copy | Ctrl+C | Apply Names... | |
| Save | Shift+F12 | Paste | Ctrl+V | Note... | |
| Save As... | F12 | Clear... | Del | Goto... | F5 |
| Save Workbook... | | Paste Special... | | Find... | Shift+F5 |
| Delete... | | Paste Link | | Replace... | |
| Print Preview | | Delete... | | Select Special... | |
| Page Setup... | | Insert... | | Show Active Cell | |
| Print... | Ctrl+Shift+F12 | Insert Object... | | Outline... | |
| Print Report... | | Fill Right | Ctrl+R | Goal Seek... | |
| Exit | Alt+F4 | Fill Down | Ctrl+D | Solver... | |
| | | | | Scenario Manager... | |

| Format | Data | Options |
|---|---|---|
| Number... | Form... | Set Print Area |
| Alignment... | Find | Set Print Titles... |
| Font... | Extract... | Set Page Break |
| Border... | Delete | Display... |
| Patterns... | Set Database | Toolbars... |
| Cell Protection... | Set Criteria | Color Palette... |
| Style... | Set Extract | Protect Document... |
| AutoFormat... | Sort... | Add-ins... |
| Row Height... | Series... | Calculation... |
| Column Width... | Table... | Workspace... |
| Justify | Parse... | Spelling... |
| Bring to Front | Consolidate... | Group Edit... |
| Send to Back | Crosstab... | Analysis Tools... |
| Group | | |
| Object Properties... | | |

| Macro | Window | Help |
|---|---|---|
| Run... | New Window | Contents F1 |
| Record... | Arrange... | Search... |
| Start Recorder | Hide | Product Support |
| Set Recorder | Unhide... | Introducing Microsoft Excel |
| Relative Record | View... | Learning Microsoft Excel |
| Assign to Object... | Split | Lotus 1-2-3... |
| Resume | Freeze Panes | Multiplan Help... |
| | Zoom... | About Microsoft Excel... |
| | √ 1 Sheet1 | |

# SYBEX *Running* **START** BOOKS

The SYBEX *Running Start* series offers busy, computer-literate people two books in one: a quick, hands-on tutorial guide to program essentials, and a comprehensive reference to commands and features.

The first half of each *Running Start* book teaches the basic operations and underlying concepts of the topic software. These lessons feature trademark SYBEX characteristics: step-by-step procedures; thoughtful, well-chosen examples; an engaging writing style; valuable Notes, Tips, and Warnings; and plenty of practical insights.

Once you've learned the basics, you're ready to start working on your own. That's where the second half of each *Running Start* book comes in. This alphabetical reference offers concise instructions for using program commands, dialog boxes, and menu options. With dictionary-style organization and headings, this half of the book is designed to give you fast access to information.

SYBEX is very interested in your reactions to the *Running Start* series. Your opinions and suggestions will help all of our readers, including yourself. Please send your comments to: SYBEX Editorial Department, 2021 Challenger Dr., Alameda, CA 94501.

# EXCEL FOR WINDOWS *Running* START

# EXCEL FOR WINDOWS™ *Running* START

STEPHEN L. NELSON

San Francisco • Paris • Düsseldorf • Soest

SYBEX®

Acquisitions Editor: David Clark
Developmental Editor: David Peal
Editor: James A. Compton
Technical Editor: Ellen Ferlazzo
Production Editor: Carolina Montilla
Book Designer: Claudia Smelser
"Running Start" Icon Designer: Alissa Feinberg
Production Artist: Charlotte Carter
Desktop Publishing Production: Claudia Smelser
Screen Graphics: John Corrigan
Proofreaders: Mark Giles, Carolina Montilla
Indexer: Anne Leach
Cover Design and Illustration: Archer Design

Screen reproductions produced with Collage Plus.

Collage Plus is a trademark of Inner Media Inc.

SYBEX is a registered trademark of SYBEX, Inc.

TRADEMARKS: SYBEX has attempted throughout this book to distinguish proprietary trademarks from descriptive terms by following the capitalization style used by the manufacturer.

SYBEX is not affiliated with any manufacturer.

Every effort has been made to supply complete and accurate information. However, SYBEX assumes no responsibility for its use, nor for any infringement of the intellectual property rights of third parties which would result from such use.

An earlier version of this book was published under the title *Learn Excel for Windows Fast!*, copyright ©1992 SYBEX Inc.
Copyright ©1993 SYBEX Inc., 2021 Challenger Drive, Alameda, CA 94501. World rights reserved. No part of this publication may be stored in a retrieval system, transmitted, or reproduced in any way, including but not limited to photocopy, photograph, magnetic or other record, without the prior agreement and written permission of the publisher.

Library of Congress Card Number: 92-85594
ISBN: 0-7821-1195-5

Manufactured in the United States of America
10 9 8 7 6 5 4 3 2 1

# ACKNOWLEDGMENTS

A lot of people worked very hard so that this book provides you, the reader, with maximum value. I know it's difficult to connect with people you've never met and, perhaps, will never meet, but you should know that these people spent days and, in some cases, weeks of their time thinking about you and how to make one part of your life—learning and using Microsoft Excel—easier. So, who are these people? Well, here is the roll of honor for *Excel for Windows Running Start*:

David Clark, acquisitions editor

David Peal, developmental editor

James Compton, copy editor

Ellen Ferlazzo, technical editor

Claudia Smelser, designer and desktop publishing specialist

Carolina Montilla, production editor

Many thanks to everyone listed above for a job well done. Also, technical editor Martin L. Moore and editor Alex Miloradovich made many contributions to the previous version of this book that have been incorporated here. Thanks also to Microsoft Corporation's Public Relations Department for providing software and information.

Stephen L. Nelson

# TABLE *of* CONTENTS

Introduction     xvii

## PART I    STEP-BY-STEP TUTORIAL

### lesson 1    GETTING STARTED WITH WORKSHEET BASICS    3

Working with the Program    4
    Starting Excel    4
    The Application Window    4
    The Document Window    4
    Moving Around Your Worksheet    6
    Finding Help When You Need It    7
Creating Your First Worksheet    7
    Entering Labels    8
    Entering Values    9
    Correcting Typing Mistakes    10
Saving Your Work    10
Exiting the Program    11
Looking Ahead    11

### lesson 2    USING FORMULAS AND FUNCTIONS    13

Retrieving Your Worksheet    14
Entering Formulas    15
    Formula Fundamentals    15
    Using Cell References    16
    Understanding Worksheet Recalculation    17
    Formula Errors    18
Using Functions    18

| | | |
|---|---|---|
| | Using Named Ranges | 20 |
| |    Creating and Using a Range Name | 20 |
| |    Range Name Rules | 23 |
| | Looking Ahead | 23 |

## lesson 3    BUILDING A FRAMEWORK OF EDITING SKILLS    25

| | |
|---|---|
| Erasing Ranges | 26 |
| Undoing Mistakes | 28 |
| Copying, Cutting, and Pasting | 28 |
|    Copying Labels and Values | 28 |
|    Copying Formulas | 30 |
|    Moving Labels, Values, and Formulas | 31 |
|    Filling Ranges | 32 |
| Inserting and Deleting Cells, Rows, and Columns | 32 |
|    The Insert Command | 32 |
|    The Delete Command | 33 |
| Using Find and Replace | 34 |
|    The Find Command | 34 |
|    The Replace Command | 34 |
| Checking Your Spelling | 35 |
| Looking Ahead | 36 |

## lesson 4    ENHANCING YOUR WORK WITH FORMATTING    37

| | |
|---|---|
| Using the Autoformat Command | 38 |
|    Selective Autoformatting | 40 |
| Working with Manual Formatting | 40 |
|    Aligning Labels and Values | 40 |
|    Assigning Formats to Numbers | 42 |
|    Changing Font Styles and Sizes | 43 |
|    Creating Borders and Shaded Cells | 45 |
|    Modifying Column and Row Size | 46 |
| Looking Ahead | 47 |

## lesson 5 — PRINTING AND MANAGING YOUR FILES — 49

Printing with Excel — 50
    Setting Up Pages — 51
    The Print Preview Command — 52
    Options Menu Print Commands — 54
Managing Your Files with Excel — 56
    Handling Multiple Files — 56
    Deleting Files — 57
    Exporting and Importing — 58
Looking Ahead — 59

## lesson 6 — PRESENTING YOUR DATA WITH CHARTS — 61

Creating and Working with Charts — 62
    Using the ChartWizard — 62
    Working with the Chart Toolbar — 68
Understanding the Different Chart Types — 69
    Using Two-dimensional and Three-dimensional Area Charts — 70
    Using Two-dimensional and Three-dimensional Bar Charts — 71
    Using Two-dimensional and Three-dimensional Column Charts — 72
    Using Two-dimensional and Three-dimensional Line Charts — 72
    Using Pie Charts — 72
    Using Radar Charts — 73
    Using Surface Charts — 74
    Using XY, or Scatter, Charts — 74
    Using Combination Charts — 74
Saving, Retrieving, and Printing Your Charts — 75
    Saving Charts as Independent Files — 75
    Printing Charts as Separate Items — 76
Looking Ahead — 76

## lesson 7 — AUTOMATING YOUR WORK WITH MACROS — 77

Recording and Running Keystroke Macros — 78
    The Record Command — 78
    The Run Command — 80

|  |  |  |
|---|---|---|
|  | Macro Recorder Tips | 81 |
|  | Writing a Command Macro | 83 |
|  | Looking Ahead | 86 |

### lesson 8   ORGANIZING INFORMATION WITH DATABASES   87

|  |  |
|---|---|
| Creating Databases | 88 |
|     Defining Your Database | 88 |
|     Entering Data | 89 |
| Working with Databases | 90 |
|     Editing Database Records | 90 |
|     Sorting Your Database | 91 |
|     Finding and Extracting Records | 93 |
| Printing, Saving, and Retrieving Database Files | 96 |
| Looking Ahead | 96 |

### lesson 9   EXCEL AND WINDOWS   97

|  |  |
|---|---|
| Running Multiple Applications | 98 |
| Understanding the Print Manager | 100 |
|     Troubleshooting with Print Manager | 100 |
| Sharing Data Using Object Linking and Embedding | 102 |
|     Embedding vs. Linking | 106 |
| Looking Ahead |  |

### PART II   ALPHABETICAL REFERENCE

|  |  |
|---|---|
| Add-Ins | 109 |
| Analysis Tools | 109 |
| Annotating Cells | 109 |
| Application Windows | 110 |
|     To Control Workspace Settings | 111 |
| Automatic Backup | 111 |
| Calculating Worksheets | 112 |
| Cell Address | 112 |
| Cell Characteristics | 112 |
| Cell Reference | 114 |

| | |
|---|---|
| Charting | 114 |
|     To Use ChartWizard | 114 |
| Clearing Data | 116 |
| Closing a File | 116 |
| Color Palette | 117 |
| Column Width | 118 |
| Consolidating Data | 119 |
| Copying Data to the Clipboard | 119 |
| Creating a New File | 119 |
| Cutting Data to the Clipboard | 120 |
| Databases | 121 |
|     To Use a Form for Data Entry | 121 |
|     To Find Database Records | 121 |
|     To Set a Database Range | 122 |
|     To Set Search Criteria | 122 |
|     To Set an Extraction Range | 122 |
|     To Extract a Database Record | 123 |
|     To Delete a Database Record | 123 |
| Deleting Columns and Rows | 123 |
| Deleting a File | 124 |
| Document Windows | 125 |
|     To Arrange Size and Position | 125 |
|     To Control the Display of Document Windows | 125 |
|     To Hide a Document Window | 126 |
|     To Unhide a Document Window | 126 |
|     To Create a New Document Window | 127 |
|     To View Document Window Formats | 127 |
|     To Zoom In and Out | 127 |
|     To Split a Window into Panes | 128 |
|     To Freeze Panes on Split Document Windows | 128 |
| Drawing Features | 128 |
| Exiting Excel | 130 |
| Files | 131 |
| Filling Cell Data into Selected Ranges | 131 |
| Finding Cell Data | 132 |
| Font Styles | 133 |
| Formatting | 134 |
|     To Align Values and Labels | 134 |
|     To Justify Text | 135 |

| | |
|---|---|
| To Use Autoformat | 136 |
| To Format Borders and Cells | 137 |
| To Format Numbers | 138 |
| To Apply Patterns and Cell Shading | 138 |
| To Apply a Style | 139 |
| Formulas | 140 |
| Goto Command | 141 |
| Graphic Objects | 141 |
|     Grouping Graphic Objects | 142 |
|     To Insert Objects in Documents | 142 |
|     To Move Objects Back and Front | 143 |
|     To Control Object Properties | 143 |
| Grouping Worksheets and Macro Sheets | 144 |
| Help | 145 |
|     Help on Excel | 145 |
|     Help for Lotus 1-2-3 Users | 146 |
|     Help for Microsoft Multiplan Users | 146 |
|     Product Support | 148 |
| Importing and Exporting Data | 148 |
|     To Export Data to Another Application | 148 |
|     To Import Data from Another Application | 148 |
|     To Parse Imported Text | 148 |
| Inserting Columns and Rows | 149 |
| Labels | 150 |
| Linking Files | 150 |
| Macros | 151 |
|     To Record a Macro | 151 |
|     To Start and Stop the Recorder | 152 |
|     To Resume Recording | 152 |
|     To Assign a Macro to an Object | 152 |
|     To Run a Macro | 152 |
|     Macro Set Recorder | 153 |
|     Relative and Absolute Recording | 153 |
| Modeling | 154 |
|     Optimization Modeling | 154 |
|     Target Value Modeling | 154 |
|     What-If Modeling | 156 |
| Object Linking and Embedding | 158 |

| | |
|---|---|
| On-Line Demonstration and Tutorial Programs | 158 |
|     To Run the Excel Demonstrations | 158 |
|     To Run the Excel Tutorial | 159 |
| Opening a File | 159 |
| Outlining Worksheet Data | 160 |
| Page Breaks | 162 |
| Page Setup | 162 |
| Pasting Data from the Clipboard | 163 |
|     To Paste All Clipboard Data | 163 |
|     To Paste Only Selected Clipboard Data | 163 |
| Pasting Functions in Formulas | 164 |
| Pasting Link Formulas | 165 |
| Printing | 166 |
|     To Print a Worksheet | 166 |
|     To Preview a Printout | 167 |
| To Print Predefined Reports | 168 |
|     To Set Print Areas | 168 |
|     To Set Print Titles | 168 |
| Q+E Application | 170 |
| Range Names | 171 |
|     To Name a Range | 171 |
|     To Apply a Range Name | 172 |
|     To Create a Range Name from a Worksheet Label | 172 |
|     To Paste a Range Name | 173 |
| Repeating the Last Command | 174 |
| Replacing Cell Data | 175 |
| Row Height | 176 |
| Saving a File | 177 |
|     To Save a File in a Workbook | 178 |
| Security | 178 |
|     Password Protection | 178 |
|     Read-Only Status | 179 |
|     Protecting Documents | 179 |
|     Cell Protection | 180 |
| Series Values | 181 |
| Showing the Active Cell | 181 |
| Sorting Worksheet Data | 181 |
| Spell-Checking Documents | 182 |

| | |
|---|---|
| Table Command Scenarios | 184 |
| Toolbar Control | 184 |
| Undoing Mistakes | 185 |
| Values | 186 |
| Windows | 187 |
| Workbooks | 187 |

*appendix* **INSTALLATION INSTRUCTIONS** **189**

Index 191

# INTRODUCTION

I'm going to make this short and sweet. You didn't buy this book for my prose. You bought it to learn Microsoft Excel for Windows, in minutes rather than days or weeks. Before you get started, there are a few things you should know to help you get the most from this book.

## HOW THIS BOOK WORKS

This book is divided into two distinct parts. Part I, the Step-by-Step Tutorial section, is a basic guide to building and working with Excel for Windows worksheets, charts, macros, and databases fast! Part II, the Alphabetical Reference section, not only supports you with detailed information as you work through the tutorial, but helps point you in the right direction as you gain skill with Excel's powerful features.

Like the other SYBEX books in this series, *Excel for Windows Running Start* employs clear, concise examples, valuable notes, tips, and warnings, and graphic features designed to enhance and speed your learning experience. An appendix guides you through the simple procedures for installing Excel.

## PART I: STEP-BY-STEP TUTORIAL

The first part of this book is organized into seven lessons, each covering a basic spreadsheet topic.

**Lesson 1:** *Getting Started with Worksheet Basics* covers the basic knowledge you'll need to begin building Excel worksheets. It reviews the geography of Excel's application and document windows, and shows you how to build and save a simple Excel worksheet.

**Lesson 2**: *Using Formulas and Functions* introduces some of Excel's most powerful features, including automatic recalculation and the ability to name cells and cell ranges for use in formulas.

**Lesson 3:** *Building a Framework of Editing Skills* shows you how to retrieve a worksheet, undo mistakes, and use Excel's basic editing features. You'll learn to work with ranges, delete and insert rows and columns, find and replace worksheet data, and check your spelling.

**Lesson 4:** *Enhancing Your Work with Formatting* explains the tools Excel provides to make your worksheets easier to read and more visually attractive. In addition to the AutoFormat feature, topics such as aligning labels and values, formatting numbers, choosing font styles and sizes, and creating borders and shaded cells are covered in detail.

**Lesson 5:** *Printing and Managing Your Files* describes how to print your documents using Excel's Page Setup, Print Preview, and Options menu commands. You'll also learn how to erase unneeded files, export and import files to and from other applications, and handle multiple files in Excel's Windows environment.

**Lesson 6:** *Presenting Your Data with Charts* introduces Excel's chart-making capabilities. You'll learn to create, save, and print charts using Excel's ChartWizard feature and the special capabilities of the Chart toolbar.

**Lesson 7:** *Automating Your Work with Macros* provides some valuable tips and basic information on creating and running simple macros with Excel's Record and Run commands. This lesson also points the way to building powerful applications from scratch with Excel's macro sheet capabilities.

**Lesson 8:** *Organizing Information with Databases* teaches you to create, edit, and work with simple databases within Excel. You'll learn to sort, find, and extract records, and to print, save, and retrieve database files.

**Lesson 9**: *Excel and Windows* discusses the environment in wich Excel operates. You'll learn about running multiple applications, working with the Print Manager, and object linking and embedding (OLE).

## PART II: ALPHABETICAL REFERENCE

Each alphabetical entry provides a brief explanation of the topic, the menu and command path, the shortcut key combination if available, and a description of how the command operation works. Cross-references and additional notes are also included when needed.

## ABOUT MICROSOFT WINDOWS

This book was written assuming a basic level of knowledge and skill in using Microsoft Windows. Before continuing, make sure you know how to start and stop Windows applications, choose commands from menus, and work with dialog boxes. These basics and this book are all you require to quickly learn how to use Excel for Windows.

# PART I

# STEP-BY-STEP TUTORIAL

# Getting Started with Worksheet Basics

**INTRODUCING**

*Starting and working with Excel*

*Creating your first worksheet*

*Saving your work and exiting the program*

With the right help, you can begin working with Excel in just a few minutes. This lesson shows how to start the program, work with Excel's windows, and create and save your first worksheet.

*Getting Started with Worksheet Basics*
**LESSON 1**

# WORKING WITH THE PROGRAM

Before you begin, make sure Excel 4 has been properly installed on your system under Windows 3.0 or later. Start your computer, run Windows, and display the Program Manager window.

> *See the Appendix for detailed information on the installation process.*

## STARTING EXCEL

To start Excel from the Windows Program Manager, switch to the Excel program group window and double-click the Excel icon. You can also highlight the icon with the arrow keys and press ↵. When Excel has started, your screen should look like Figure 1.1.

## THE APPLICATION WINDOW

The Microsoft Excel title bar and menu bar are at the top of the application window. The tool bar, located just below the menu bar, is a series of buttons that allow for faster selection of frequently used menu commands. All the tool bar buttons are identified on the inside covers of this book, and each one appears in the margin the first time it's used in a lesson.

The formula bar displays the data you enter into your worksheet. At the bottom of the application window, the status bar displays a variety of messages such as "Ready" to enter data.

## THE DOCUMENT WINDOW

The document window is the area between the formula bar and the status bar. When you start Excel, it automatically opens an empty worksheet file named Sheet1.XLS.

4

*Working with the Program*

**FIGURE 1.1:**
The Excel application window with a blank worksheet

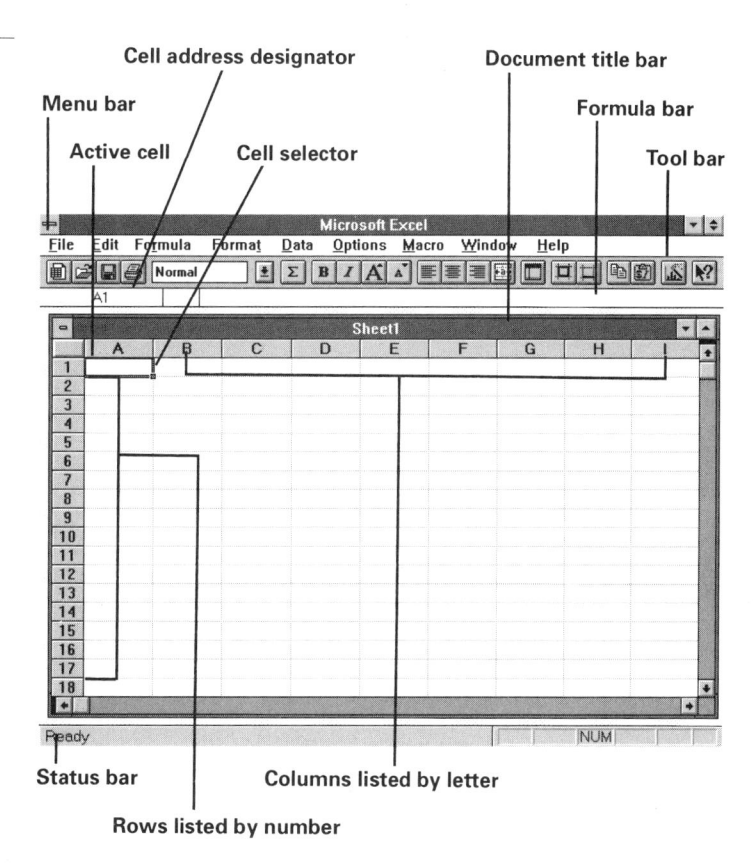

[Figure 1.1 shows the Excel application window with callouts labeling: Cell address designator, Document title bar, Menu bar, Formula bar, Active cell, Cell selector, Tool bar, Status bar, Rows listed by number, Columns listed by letter.]

**Rows and Cells** Under the title bar, the column border identifies each of the 256 columns available for your worksheet with a letter of the alphabet. Excel uses double letters for columns 27 through 256. The left edge of the document window identifies each row in your worksheet with a number. An Excel worksheet can have up to 16,384 rows. The intersection of a column and row is called a *cell*. Each cell has an address consisting of the column letter and row number. The cell in the top left corner of the worksheet is cell A1.

A dark outline called the *cell selector* identifies the active cell. Figure 1.1 shows the cell selector in cell A1. The address of the active cell also appears on the left-hand side of the formula bar.

**5**

*Getting Started with Worksheet Basics*
**LESSON 1**

## MOVING AROUND YOUR WORKSHEET

With up to 256 columns by 16,384 rows, a worksheet can get pretty big. Excel provides four ways of moving and displaying the document window around the worksheet area. Practice moving the window through your worksheet using each of the following methods. Discover the techniques that work best for you.

**With Scroll Bars**  If you have a mouse, you can use the vertical and horizontal scroll bars along the right and bottom edges of the document window to move through your worksheet. Just click inside the scroll bars to move a screen at a time. Click the arrows to move one row or column.

> *Scroll bars are a basic element of the Windows interface. For more information on how to use them, refer to the Microsoft Windows User Guide.*

**With Navigation Keys**  The standard navigation keys, PageUp and PageDn, move through your worksheet up and down a screen at a time. When you hold down the Ctrl key and then press PageUp or PageDn, your worksheet moves right or left a screen at a time.

**Using the Cell Selector**  Excel moves the worksheet as you move the cell selector. You can move the cell selector in all directions with the arrow keys, to the right with the Tab key, and to the left by holding Shift while you press the Tab key.

**Using the Goto Command**  The Goto command lets you move the cell selector to a designated cell address. Choose the Goto command from the Formula menu or press F5 to display the Goto dialog box shown in Figure 1.2. Enter the cell address in the Reference text box and select OK.

   If you're working with named cells or ranges, their names appear in the Goto list box. You can move the cell selector to a named cell or range by choosing it from the list and selecting OK.

6

**FIGURE 1.2:**

The Goto Dialog Box

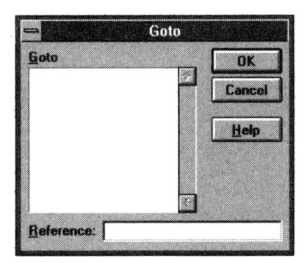

*See Lesson 2 and Range Names in the Reference for more information on using cell and range names.*

## FINDING HELP WHEN YOU NEED IT

Excel uses the standard Windows Help application. To start Help, choose the Contents command from the Help menu or select the Help command button on the tool bar.

*For help with Help, refer to the Help entry in the Reference section of this book.*

## CREATING YOUR FIRST WORKSHEET

Excel lets you enter labels, values, and formulas in the cells of your worksheet. Let's construct a simple budgeting worksheet. (Although you don't need to work through this example or others in this book to learn the essential procedures, doing so will allow you to practice using Excel without worrying about inadvertently losing or damaging valuable real-world data.)

*Getting Started with Worksheet Basics*
**LESSON 1**

## ENTERING LABELS

*Labels* are simply any information entered into a worksheet that you don't want to manipulate arithmetically. They often identify the values that are subject to calculation, so you normally enter them as the first stage in setting up a worksheet. Usually, labels are pieces of text, such as the expense categories in a budgeting worksheet or the employee names in a payroll worksheet. However, they can also be numbers that won't be used arithmetically, such as telephone numbers or part or project ID numbers.

Entering labels is a three-step process. We can demonstrate it by entering the label shown in cell A1 in Figure 1.3. To enter this label, you would follow these steps:

**1.** Move the cell selector to the desired location (in this case, cell A1) using the mouse or the arrow keys.

**2.** Type the label (here, **Advertising**). As you do, Excel displays what you've typed on the formula bar. It also adds the Enter command button, labeled with a check mark, and the Cancel command button, labeled with an X, to the formula bar.

**3.** Next, you move the label from the formula bar to the active cell. To do this, you select the Enter command button, press ↵, or move the cell selector. When you do, Excel displays the label in its cell (A1).

If you're following along on-line, repeat the same steps to enter the labels shown in cells A2 through A6. As Figure 1.3 shows, Excel aligns your labels to the left in each cell, and allows long labels to spill over into adjacent cells if they are unoccupied.

**FIGURE 1.3:**
Your first worksheet with labels entered.

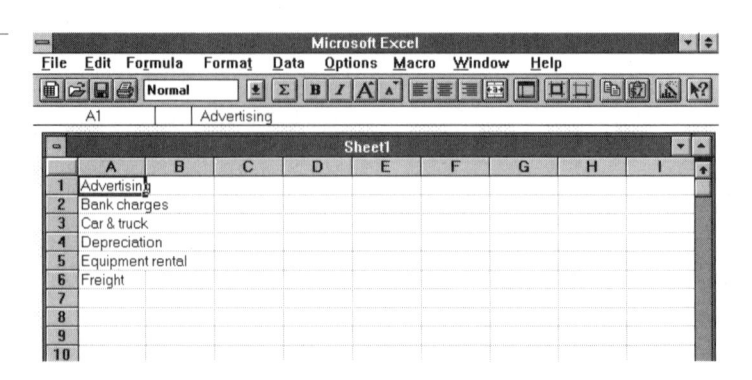

## ENTERING VALUES

*Values* are numbers you want to add, subtract, multiply, divide, and use in formulas and functions. In a budgeting worksheet, for example, you would need to enter the budgeted amounts as values. Figure 1.4 shows the values, or amounts, entered opposite each of your worksheet labels.

To enter values, you use the ten number keys (on either the main keyboard or the numeric keypad) and the period and hyphen keys. Use the period key to show decimal places. Use the hyphen key to identify negative values. (The hyphen represents a minus sign.)

To enter values, you use the same three-step process as you do to enter labels. For example, to enter the value 500 shown in cell C1, you would follow these steps:

1. Move the cell selector to the desired cell (here, C1) using the mouse or the arrow keys.

2. Type the value (500). As you do, Excel displays the number on formula bar. It also adds the Enter and Cancel command buttons to the formula bar.

3. Move the value 500 from the formula bar to the active cell by selecting the Enter command button, pressing ↵, or moving the cell selector. Excel displays the value 500 in cell C1.

To enter the rest of the values shown in Figure 1.4, you would repeat the steps for each value.

**FIGURE 1.4:**
Your worksheet with labels and values entered.

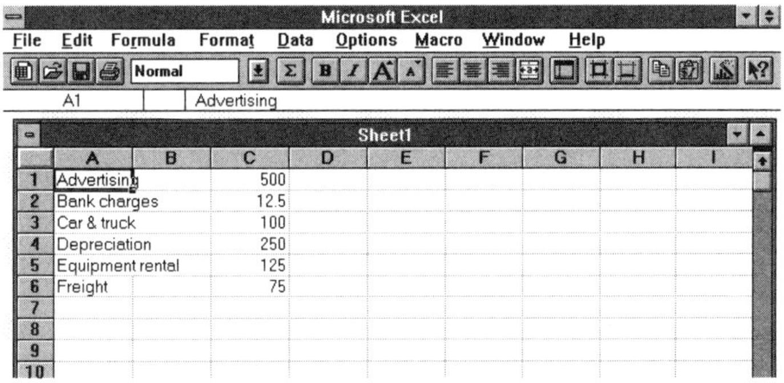

*Getting Started with Worksheet Basics*
**LESSON 1**

> **NOTE**
> 
> *Excel displays values too large to fit a single cell in scientific notation. The number 123456789 appears as 1.23E+08, and .0000001 as 1E–07. Excel doesn't display characters such as dollar signs, percentage symbols, or commas when you enter them in a cell, but uses them to format those values. Excel also has a variety of date and time formatting options. Refer to Lesson 4 for more information on formatting.*

## CORRECTING TYPING MISTAKES

If you make any typing mistakes before moving a label or value from the formula bar to the cell, use the Backspace key to erase characters to the left of the insertion point and then retype the correct data. You can also reposition the insertion point with the arrow keys and erase characters to the right with the Delete key. If you don't want to enter the data shown on the formula bar into the active cell, select the Cancel command button or press Esc.

If you make a mistake but don't realize it until after moving the label or value from the formula bar to the cell, move the cell selector to the cell holding the erroneous label or value. Click on the formula bar or press F2 (Edit). Excel displays the label or value in the active cell on the formula bar. Now use the Backspace key to erase characters to the left of the insertion point and then retype the correct data (or reposition the insertion point with the arrow keys, erase characters to the right with the Delete key, and then retype the correct data). When the formula bar shows the correct label or value, move it to the active cell by moving the cell selector, selecting the Enter command button, or pressing ↵.

## SAVING YOUR WORK

When you first save a worksheet, you must give it a name and tell Excel where to store it. If you've worked with other Windows applications, you will find the procedure quite familiar. We can demonstrate it using the sample worksheet.

1. Choose File ➤ Save As. Excel displays the dialog box shown in Figure 1.5.
2. Select a drive, if necessary, from the Drives list.
3. Use the directories list to choose the directory or subdirectory.

**FIGURE 1.5:**
The File Save As dialog box.

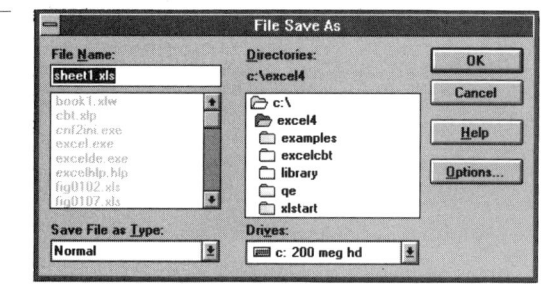

4. Move to the File Name text box and type a name, but don't add an extension—Excel automatically adds the extension .XLS to all worksheet files. If you're following the example, name the file BUDGET.
5. Choose OK.

Once you've saved and named a worksheet file you can use the Save command on the File menu or the Save File tool on the tool bar for subsequent saves.

> **TIP** *The Options command button on the File ➤ Save As dialog box opens the door to some useful features such as automatic file back up, passwords, and read-only files.*

# EXITING THE PROGRAM

Once you've saved your work, you can exit Excel by choosing File ➤ Exit. Windows closes the Excel application window and redisplays the Excel 4 program group window.

# LOOKING AHEAD

Lesson 1 helped you get off to a fast start by showing you how to create and save your first Excel worksheet. For more information on the subjects introduced in this lesson, see the following topics in the Reference section of this book:

Document Window

**11**

*Getting Started with Worksheet Basics*
**LESSON 1**

    Help

    On-Line Demonstration and Tutorial Programs

    Range Names

    Saving Files

    Security

With what you already know, you're well on your way to acquiring the knowledge you need to use Excel. To employ Excel productively as an analytical tool, however, you also must know how to use formulas and functions—the subject of the next lesson.

# Using Formulas and Functions

**INTRODUCTING**

*Retrieving saved worksheets*
*Using formulas*
*Using functions*
*Naming ranges*

Much of Excel's power stems from its ability to perform calculations on the values you've stored in a worksheet—something you do with formulas and functions. This lesson shows how to construct formulas, use Excel's predefined formulas, or functions, and use range names in formulas. You'll also see how to retrieve previously saved worksheets.

*Using Formulas and Functions*
**LESSON 2**

# RETRIEVING YOUR WORKSHEET

In this lesson you'll use the BUDGET.XLS worksheet you created and saved in Lesson 1 to learn about formulas. First, make sure Excel is running. To retrieve the worksheet, follow these steps

1. Select File ➤ Open or the Open File tool from the tool bar. Excel displays the File Open dialog box shown in Figure 2.1.

2. Specify the disk you saved your worksheet on by activating the Drives drop-down list box and selecting the correct drive.

3. Use the Directories list box to select the directory in which your file is stored.

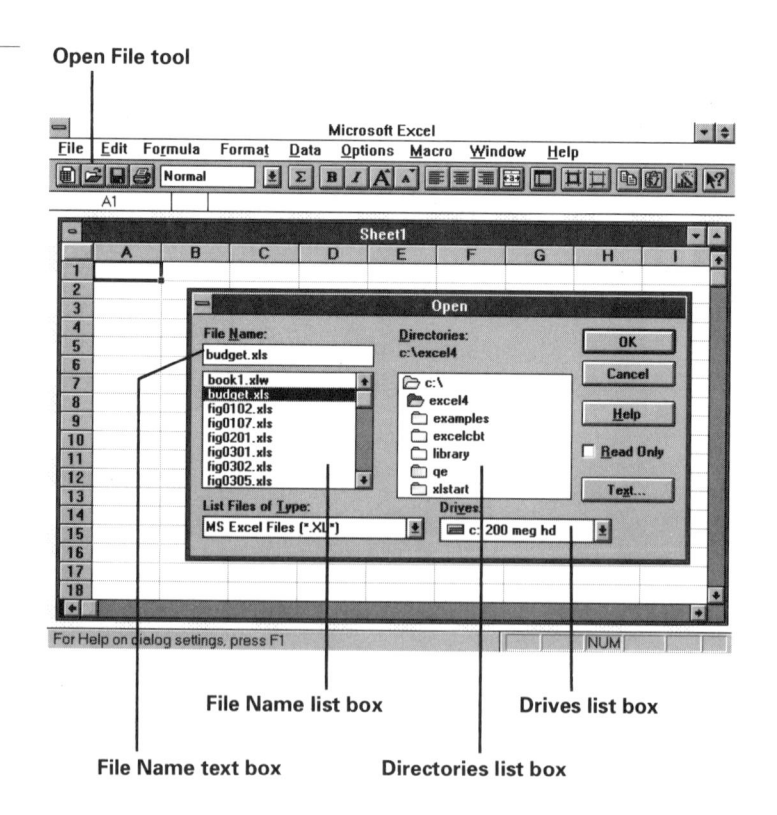

**FIGURE 2.1:**
The File Open dialog box

4. Select the BUDGET.XLS worksheet file from the File Name list box or enter its file name in the text box.

5. Select the OK command button to retrieve your worksheet.

# ENTERING FORMULAS

Excel calculates formulas automatically. You enter them into worksheet cells via the formula bar, as you do with labels and values. In the worksheet cell, however, Excel displays not the formula but its result. For example, if you enter a formula that says to add 4 and 2, Excel displays the result, 6, and not the actual formula.

## FORMULA FUNDAMENTALS

Formulas must begin with the equal sign (=); that's how Excel distinguishes them from values and labels. You can construct formulas that subtract, multiply, divide, and exponentiate. The − symbol means subtraction, the * symbol multiplication, the / symbol division, and the ^ symbol exponential operation. The following formulas show the different mathematical operators and the results they return.

| FORMULA ENTERED | RESULT DISPLAYED IN CELL |
| --- | --- |
| =4+2 | 6 |
| =4-2 | 2 |
| =4*2 | 8 |
| =4/2 | 2 |
| =4^2 | 16 |

To build more complicated formulas, you need to recognize the standard rules of operator precedence. Excel performs arithmetic operations in the following order:

- Exponential operations first
- Multiplication and division second
- Addition and subtraction third

*Using Formulas and Functions*
**LESSON 2**

For example, in the equation, =1+2*3^4, Excel first raises 3 to the fourth power to calculate the result 81. It then multiplies this value by 2 to get 162. Finally, it adds 1 to this value to get 163.

To override these rules, use parentheses. Excel first performs the function most deeply nested. The following formulas show how Excel calculates the formula =1+2*3^4 with and without parentheses:

| FORMULA ENTERED | RESULT DISPLAYED IN CELL |
| --- | --- |
| =1+2*3^4 | 163 |
| =(1+2)*3^4 | 243 |
| =((1+2)*3)^4 | 6561 |

## USING CELL REFERENCES

In the BUDGET.XLS worksheet, you could total the budgeted expenses by entering the formula =500+12.5+100+250+125+75 into cell C8. There is, however, a practical problem with this approach: You would need to rewrite the formula each time any of the values changed. What-if analysis (see Modeling in the Reference) would be virtually impossible.

Because this approach is unwieldy, Excel also allows you to use cell references in formulas. When a formula includes a cell reference, Excel uses the value that cell contains. For example, to add the budgeted amounts on your budgeting worksheet using a formula with cell references, follow these steps:

1. Move the cell selector to C8.
2. Type =C1+C2+C3+C4+C5+C6.
3. Select the Enter command button or press ↵.

*Entering Formulas*

> *You edit formulas the same way you edit values and labels. Move the cell selector to the cell holding the formula. Click on the Formula bar or press F2, the Edit key. Edit the formula as necessary. Then, when the formula is correct, move it from the formula bar back to the cell by moving the cell selector, selecting the Enter command button, or pressing ↵.*

Once you've moved the formula to the cell, Excel calculates it. Notice in Figure 2.2 that the formula appears on the formula bar and its result in the worksheet cell.

> *If you're working through these lessons, save BUDGET.XLS after entering the total budget formula into cell C8. In future lessons, you'll reuse this worksheet.*

**FIGURE 2.2:**
Your worksheet with formula entered and displayed result.

## UNDERSTANDING WORKSHEET RECALCULATION

As you edit your worksheet, Excel automatically updates the formulas and recalculates the result. For example, in the budgeting worksheet, if you change the value in cell C1 from 500 to 600, Excel recalculates any formulas that use the value stored in cell C1. In the budgeting worksheet, Excel recalculates the formula in cell C8 so it returns the value 1162.5—an increase of one hundred.

In simple worksheets like the one shown in Figure 2.2, recalculation takes place so quickly you won't even be aware it's occurring. In larger worksheets with dozens or hundreds of formulas, however, recalculation is much slower. The mouse pointer changes to the familiar Windows hourglass symbol when recalculation takes place. If you resume work, Excel suspends recalculation until you're finished. The word *Calculate* appears on the status bar when your worksheet needs to be recalculated.

You can force recalculation by pressing F9 or choosing Options ➤ Calculation and selecting the Calculate Now command button.

## FORMULA ERRORS

It's possible to build an illogical or unsolvable formula. When you do, Excel displays an error message in the cell rather than calculating the result. The error message, which begins with the # symbol, describes the error. Suppose, for example, that you enter the formula =1/0 into a cell. Because division by zero is an undefined mathematical operation, Excel can't solve the formula. To alert you to this, it would display the error message #DIV/0!.

Another common error is a circular reference. It occurs when two or more formulas indirectly depend on one another to achieve a result. For example, if the formula in cell A1 is =A2 and the formula in cell A2 is =SUM(A1:M1), A1 depends on A2 and A2 depends on A1. Excel identifies circular references by displaying the word "Circ" on the status bar and showing the address of the cell whose formula completed the "circle."

To fix a formula error, you edit the erroneous formula using the same techniques as with label and value editing.

> **NOTE:** When a formula refers to a cell that contains an erroneous formula, both formulas return the error message. For example, if cell A1 attempts to divide by zero and cell A2 refers to cell A1, cell A2 also returns the error message #DIV/0!.

## USING FUNCTIONS

Excel provides more than 300 standard formulas, called functions, that can provide a shortcut to constructing complicated or lengthy formulas. In general, a function accepts input values, or arguments, then makes some calculation and returns a resulting value.

Excel provides financial, statistical, mathematical, trigonometric, and even engineering functions. In fact, there's a very good chance that Excel already provides a simple-to-use function for any standard formula that you want to construct. For example, rather than adding your budgeted amounts by entering the formula =C1+C2+C3+C4+C5+C6, you can use the function formula =SUM(C1:C6).

Each function has a name that describes its operation. The function that adds values is named SUM, for example, and the function that calculates an arithmetic mean, or average, is named AVERAGE.

Most functions require arguments, or input values, which you enclose in parentheses. If a function uses or accepts more than a single argument, separate the arguments with commas. The ROUND function, for example, rounds a specified value to a specified number of decimal places. To round the value 5.75 to the nearest tenth, you would use the function shown below:

=ROUND(5.75,1)

Even if a function doesn't require arguments, you still need to include the parentheses. For example, the function PI returns the mathematical constant Pi. The function needs no arguments, but you still need to enter it as =PI().

Functions can use values, formulas, and even other functions as arguments. If entered into the budgeting worksheet shown in Figure 2.2, for example, each of the following functions returns the same result, 1062.5.

=SUM(C1:C6)

=SUM(C1,C2,C3,C4,C5,C6)

=SUM(500,12.5,100,250,125,75)

=SUM(SUM(C1),SUM(12.5),SUM(C3),SUM(C4),SUM(C5),SUM(C6))

> *To display a list of the Excel functions, choose the Paste Function command from the Formula menu. See Pasting Formulas in Functions in the Reference for details.*

Incidentally, because summing is such a common spreadsheet operation, Excel provides an Autosum button on the toolbar; you can use it to enter a cell formula in the active cell of a contiguous range of cells.

*Using Formulas and Functions*
**LESSON 2**

# USING NAMED RANGES

In our small sample worksheet, it's not too difficult to remember that cell C1 contains the advertising expenses, C2 the bank charges, and so on. In the real world, however, Excel worksheets can be much more complex, and keeping track of what each cell represents becomes correspondingly more difficult. Wouldn't it be nice if, instead of referring to cell C1 in a formula, you could refer to Advertising? You can, by using named ranges. A range is simply any rectangular area of the worksheet, such as a single cell, a two-cell by two-cell square, a two-cell by four-cell rectangle, or even the entire worksheet.

To make working with Excel easier, you can name ranges and then use the name of the range in place of the range address. This feature makes formula construction and review easier. For example, if you named cells C1, C2, C3, C4, C5 and C6 Advertising, Bank, Car, Depreciation, Equipment, and Freight, the following formulas would be identical:

=C1+C2+C3+C4+C5+C6

=Advertising+Bank+Car+Depreciation+Equipment+Freight

## CREATING AND USING A RANGE NAME

You can also use multiple-cell ranges as function arguments. If in the budgeting worksheet the range C1:C6 is named Budget, you can use that name in place of the range definition C1:C6.

The basic procedure for creating and using a range name is this:

**1.** Select the range of cells to be named.

**2.** Open the Formula ➤ Define Name dialog box.

**3.** Enter a name and give the OK.

**4.** If there are existing formulas that refer to the range, edit them to use the name instead.

*Using Named Ranges*

> **TIP** *You can use the Find ➤ Replace dialog box to have Excel make the changes for you automatically. See Replacing Cell Data in the Reference for details.*

To try out the range naming procedure in detail, you can use the BUDGET.XLS worksheet and take the following steps:

1. Select the range C1:C6 by clicking on cell C1 and then dragging the mouse to C6. To indicate the selected range, Excel darkens its cells, as shown in Figure 2.3.

2. Select Formula ➤ Define Name. Excel displays the Define Name dialog box, as shown in Figure 2.4. The Refers To text box shows the range you

**FIGURE 2.3:**
A selected worksheet range.

**FIGURE 2.4:**
The Define Name dialog box.

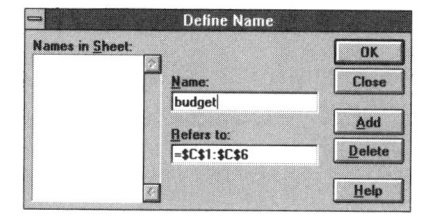

*Using Formulas and Functions*
**LESSON 2**

selected before choosing the Define Name command. If you've previously defined range names, they appear in the Names in Sheet list box.

3. Enter the range name BUDGET in the Name text box.
4. Select OK. Excel names the range C1:C6 BUDGET and it removes the Define Name dialog box.
5. Move the cell selector to cell C8.
6. Replace the existing formula in cell C8, =C1+C2+C3+C4+C5+C6, with the function =SUM(BUDGET). To do this, simply type the new function and then select the Enter command button or press ↵.

Figure 2.5 shows the BUDGET.XLS worksheet after modifying the formula to use a function and a range name.

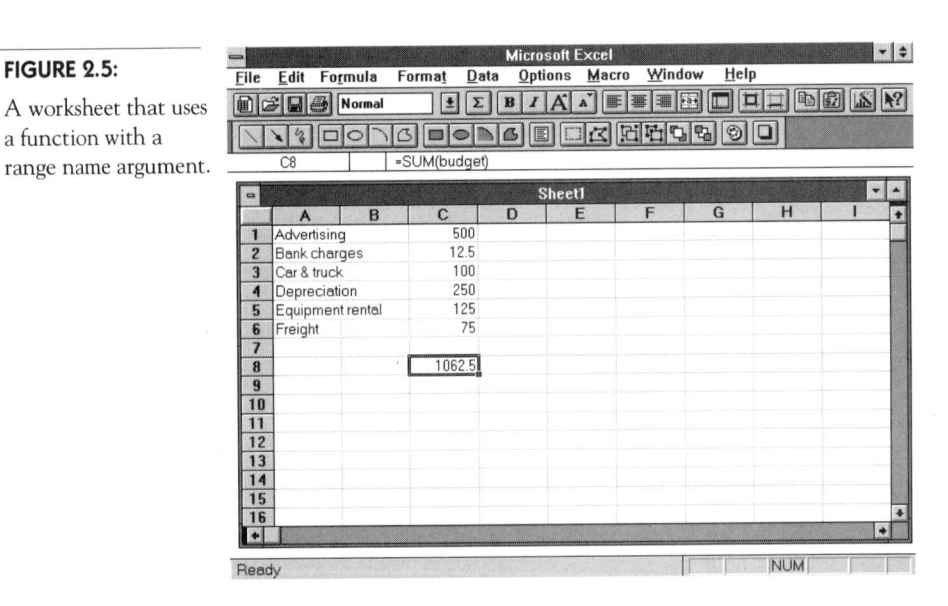

**FIGURE 2.5:**
A worksheet that uses a function with a range name argument.

22

> *Range names are useful in formulas and functions, but that's not their only use. Once you name a range, you can use the name in place of the range definition whenever Excel asks you for a range. For example, you can use the Goto command to move the cell selector to a cell. Rather than enter a cell address, you could enter a range name.*

## RANGE NAME RULES

Range names, as you have learned, make it easy to refer to cells and multiple-cell ranges. In naming ranges, however, keep in mind several rules:

- Range names must begin with a letter, not a number.
- Range names cannot include spaces.
- Range names shouldn't look like cell addresses or function names.

The following range names are valid—and descriptive.

    BUDGET
    EXPENSES
    SALES1993

The following range names are invalid, however, because they each violate one of the range naming rules:

    C1
    SUM
    1993SALES

## LOOKING AHEAD

Lesson 2 described one of Excel's most important and most powerful features: its ability to arithmetically manipulate data you've stored in a worksheet. In fact, with what you've learned so far, you can now construct extremely powerful and useful worksheet models.

*Using Formulas and Functions*
**LESSON 2**

For further information on these subjects and some of Excel's advanced features, see the following topics in the Reference section of this book:

Analysis Tools

Calculating Worksheets

Modeling

Opening a File

Pasting Functions in Formulas

Range Names

Series Values

Table Command Scenarios

Excel also provides some powerful tools for editing and enhancing your worksheets. Lesson 3 will help you quickly build a solid framework of editing skills.

# 3

# BUILDING A FRAMEWORK OF EDITING SKILLS

**INTRODUCING**

*Erasing Ranges*

*Undoing your mistakes*

*Copying, cutting and pasting cell contents*

*Inserting and deleting cells, rows, and columns*

*Using the find and replace commands*

*Spell-checking your worksheet*

Excel has many helpful commands such as Clear, Copy, Paste, Cut, Fill, Insert, Delete, Find, Replace, Undo, and Spelling that make editing your worksheets easier and more efficient. If you're following along on-line, retrieve your BUDGET.XLS worksheet, and we'll explore each of these helpful tools.

*Building a Framework of Editing Skills*
**LESSON 3**

# ERASING RANGES

You can erase single-cell and multiple-cell ranges quickly and easily. Erasing a range removes its content and formatting. To erase range A6:C6 in your worksheet, for example, you would follow these steps:

1. Select the range A6:C6 with the navigation keys or the mouse.
2. Press the Del key or choose Edit ➤ Clear. Excel displays the Clear dialog box shown in Figure 3.1. Four erasure options are listed:

| | |
|---|---|
| Formulas | The default, erases data in the selected range but leaves any formatting. |
| Formats | Erases formatting but leaves contents. |
| Notes | Erases notes created with the Formula ➤ Note command. |
| All | Erases everything in the range. |

**FIGURE 3.1:**
Range A6:C6 selected and the Clear dialog box

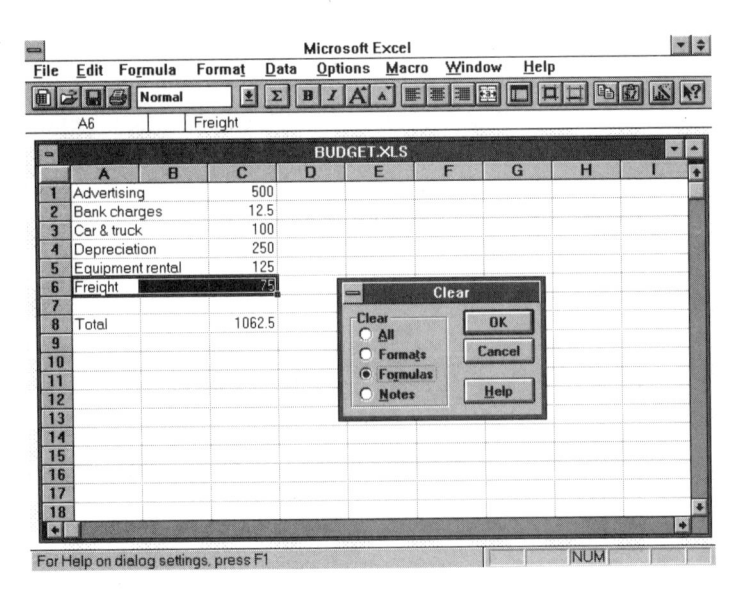

26

*Erasing Ranges*

> *See Lesson 4 for information on formatting worksheets, and the Reference entry Annotating Cells for information on adding notes.*

**3.** Press Enter or select OK. Excel clears the label in cell A6 and the value in cell C6. Figure 3.2 shows the sample worksheet with the range A6:C6 cleared.

> *After you erase the contents of a cell used in formulas in a range, you may want to edit formulas that refer to erased cells. The Find command, discussed later in this lesson, will help you locate the references.*

> *Pressing the right mouse button displays a Shortcuts menu of frequently used commands such as Clear, Copy, Paste, Cut, Insert, and Delete. As you practice the editing tasks in this lesson, use the Shortcuts menu to build your level of speed and efficiency.*

**FIGURE 3.2:**
The worksheet with the range A6:C6 cleared.

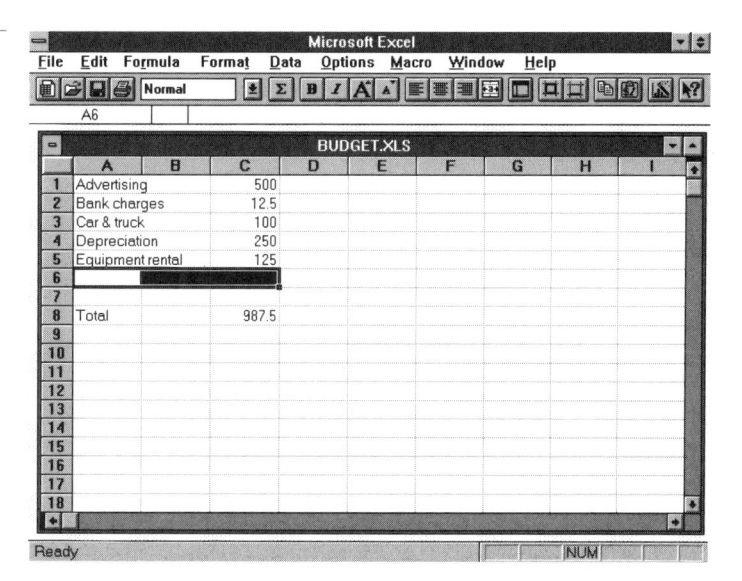

27

*Building a Framework of Editing Skills*
**LESSON 3**

# UNDOING MISTAKES

If you make a mistake entering data or editing your worksheet, you can use the Edit menu's Undo command to reverse the effects of your last action. You can even undo an undo operation. Just remember that Undo can reverse only your last action.

To undo your erasure, choose Edit ➤ Undo. As long as you choose Undo immediately after choosing Clear, Excel restores the cleared labels and values. Your budgeting worksheet should again look like the one shown in Figure 3.1.

**WARNING**
*Undo cannot undo everything. It won't undo the File Delete, Data Delete, and Data Extract commands.*

# COPYING, CUTTING, AND PASTING

You can copy or cut the contents of cells and ranges, and paste them into other locations. This means you don't have to repeatedly type a label, value or formula. You just type the entry once and then copy or move it.

## COPYING LABELS AND VALUES

You copy labels and values in the same way:

1. Select the range to be copied.
2. Choose Edit ➤ Copy (or Shortcuts ➤ Copy), or use the Copy tool on the toolbar.
3. Select a destination range.
4. Choose Edit (or Shortcuts) ➤ Paste, or press Shift and choose the Paste Formats tool on the toolbar.

To illustrate how you copy labels and values, suppose that the numbers shown in column C of the budgeting worksheet represent the budgeted expenses for January and that the same figures are projected for February and March. Rather than re-enter the same values, you could copy the values already stored in column C.

*Copying, Cutting, and Pasting*

To copy the values in the range C1:C5, you would follow these steps:

1. Select the range C1:C5 by clicking on cell C1 and dragging the mouse to cell C5.
2. Choose Edit ➤ Copy, or press the mouse's right button to display the shortcuts menu and choose Copy from it. Excel displays a flashing marquee around the range selected for copying.
3. Select the entire destination range, D1:E5, or just the first row of the range, D1:E1. To select either range, click on D1 and then drag the mouse to the other corner of the range—either E5 or E1.
4. Choose Edit (or Shortcuts) ➤ paste. Excel pastes the contents and format of the copied cells in the selected location. In this example, Excel pastes the values in cells C1:C5 into the range D1:E5.

Figure 3.3 shows how your worksheet should look after the range has been copied. When you select a destination range that is larger by a number of exact sizes than the copied range (as we've done here), Excel will automatically duplicate the original range as needed to fill the destination range.

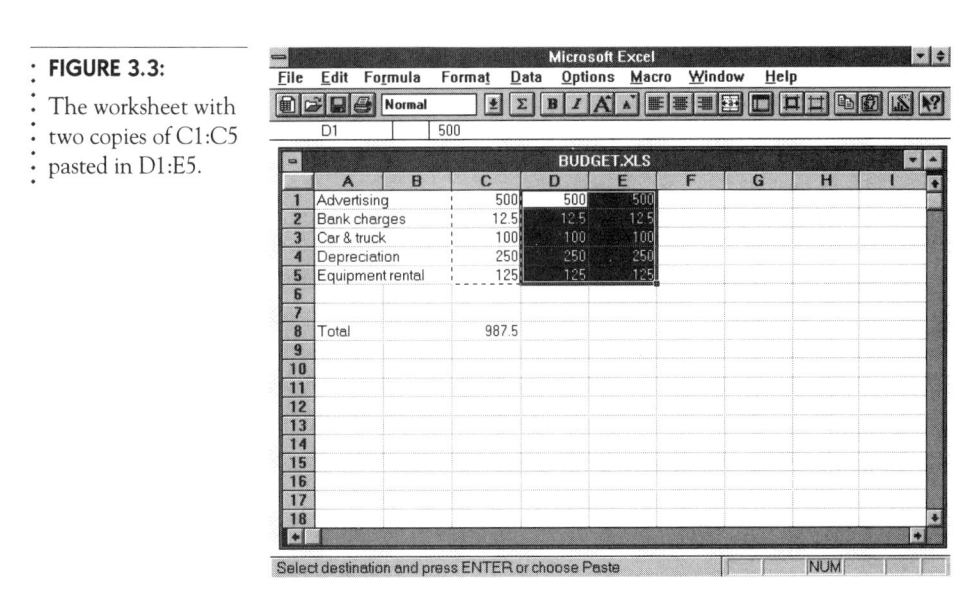

**FIGURE 3.3:**

The worksheet with two copies of C1:C5 pasted in D1:E5.

**29**

*Building a Framework of Editing Skills*
**LESSON 3**

> *If you paste a copy of a single-cell range into a multiple-cell range, the contents of the cell are duplicated in each cell in the destination range. You don't need to select the top left corner of the destination range unless you're pasting a copy of a multiple-cell range into another range of the same size.*

## COPYING FORMULAS

When you copy labels and values, Excel just duplicates the contents of the copied cell or cells and pates the data into the selected range. When you copy a formula, however, Excel adjusts any cell references used in the formula. We can illustrate this important operation by copying the formula in cell C8—=C1+C2+C3+C4+C5—into cells D8 and E8, just as we copied the values summed by that formula to create a three-month budget with the same expenses in each month. To do this, you would follow these steps:

1. Select the range C8 by moving the cell selector to it.

2. Choose Edit (or Shortcuts) ➤ Copy. Excel displays a flashing marquee around cell C8—the range you selected for copying.

3. Select the destination range D8:E8 by clicking on D8 and then dragging the mouse pointer to cell E8.

4. Choose Edit (or Shortcuts) ➤ Paste. Excel pastes the formula =D1+D2+D3+D4+D5 into cell D8 and the formula =E1+E2+E3+E4+E5 into cell E8. Figure 3.4 shows the worksheet after copying the formula. Notice that the adjusted formula in cell D8 appears on the formula bar.

The formula changes that Excel makes aren't a mistake. Excel assumes—unless you tell it otherwise—that the cell references in your formulas are *relative*. When Excel copies and pastes a formula with relative cell references, it adjusts them. If you copy the formula =C1+C2+C3+C4+C5 from cell C8 and paste it into cell D8, for example, Excel assumes that the formula should now sum values in the D column. Because the formula is still in the same row, however, Excel doesn't adjust the row numbers used in the cell references that make up the formulas.

If you copied and pasted the formula in cell C8 into the same column but a different row, Excel would adjust the row numbers used in the formula's cell references. It wouldn't adjust the column letters used, however.

**FIGURE 3.4:**
The worksheet after copying the formula in cell C8 into cells D8 and E8.

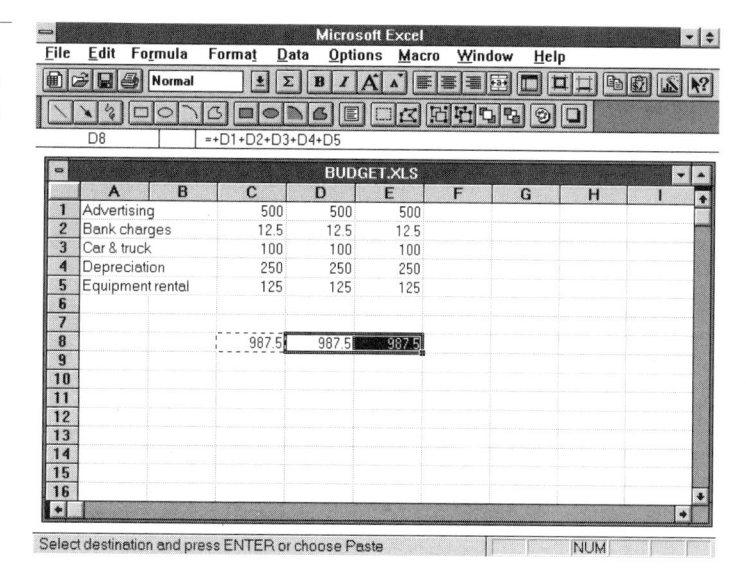

To prevent Excel from automatically adjusting the relative references of copied formulas, you can make them *absolute*. Simply place a dollar sign ($) in front of the column and row references you wish to retain as absolute.

For example, to tell Excel not to adjust the cell references in the formula =C1+C2+C3+C4+C5 if it is copied, you would edit the formula to read =$C$1+$C$2+$C$3+$C$4+$C$5. If you want Excel to adjust row numbers but not column letters, edit the formula to read =$C1+$C2+$C3+$C4+$C5. If you want Excel to adjust column letters but not row numbers, edit the formula to =C$1+C$2+C$3+C$4+C$5.

# MOVING LABELS, VALUES, AND FORMULAS

To move, rather than copy, a selected range, you follow the same procedure that we just outlined, but choose the Cut command instead of the Copy command. Excel removes ("cuts") the selected range from its original location; you can then paste it into a new location. Using this technique, you can move labels, values, and formulas.

Note that when you move a formula, Excel *doesn't* adjust the relative references used in the moved formula.

*Building a Framework of Editing Skills*
**LESSON 3**

## FILLING RANGES

The Edit menu's Fill Right and Fill Down commands let you copy a label, value or formula either vertically or horizontally into adjacent cells. To copy across a row or down a column, select first the cell you want to copy and then the cells you want to fill. Then choose the Fill Down or Fill Right command from the Edit menu. If you press the Shift key and then access the Edit menu, Excel displays the Fill Left and Fill Up commands.

> **TIP**
> If you take the time to experiment with these commands and use your sample worksheet, be sure to retain a version of BUDGET.XLS that resembles Figure 3.4. We'll be using this worksheet in subsequent exercises.

## INSERTING AND DELETING CELLS, ROWS, AND COLUMNS

Excel lets you insert and delete cells, rows, and columns on your worksheet with speed and efficiency. You can easily delete what you no longer need, or insert new items between existing entries when you need to expand your worksheet.

### THE INSERT COMMAND

To insert a row, click on any cell in the row below where you want a row inserted. The choose Edit (or Shortcut) ➤ Insert. To insert a column, first click on any cell in the column to the right of where you want a column inserted.

To insert a cell in a column, select the cell above where the new cell should go. To insert a cell in a row, select the cell to the left of where you want the cell inserted.

When you choose the Insert command, Excel displays the Insert dialog box shown in Figure 3.5.

Mark the Entire Row or Entire Column option buttons to insert these items, or the Shift Cells Right or Shift Cells Down buttons to insert cells. When you've marked the appropriate option button, select OK.

**FIGURE 3.5:**
The Insert dialog box.

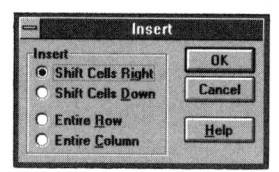

## THE DELETE COMMAND

To delete a cell, row, or column, click on the specific cell, or any cell in the row or column you wish to delete, and choose the Delete command from the Edit menu or the Shortcuts menu. Excel displays the dialog box shown in Figure 3.6.

To complete the operation, mark the appropriate option buttons and select OK.

> *A faster way to insert or delete one or more complete rows or columns is to select and highlight the rows or columns by clicking on the numbers or letters displayed on the worksheet borders, and then choosing the command. Remember that Excel inserts rows above the first selected row, and columns to the left of the first selected column. Cells are inserted to the left of selected cells in a row and above selected cells in a column.*

Excel attempts to adjust the cell references and range definitions used in formulas for row and column insertions and deletions. For example, if in Figure 3.4 you inserted a row above the row labeled Advertising, Excel adjusts the formula moved from cell C8 to cell C9 so it reads =C2+C3+C4+C5+C6. If you delete a cell referenced in a formula, however, Excel replaces the formula's cell reference with the error message #REF, indicating that the formula originally referenced a now-deleted cell.

**FIGURE 3.6:**
The Delete dialog box.

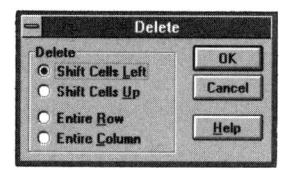

**33**

*Building a Framework of Editing Skills*
**LESSON 3**

# USING FIND AND REPLACE

Excel provides two commands that search your worksheet for specific entries. The Find command simply locates what you're looking for. The Replace command not only finds it, but gives you the option of replacing it with a new label, value, or formula.

## THE FIND COMMAND

To search your worksheet and locate specific entries, choose the Find command on the Formula or Shortcut menus. Excel displays the dialog box shown in Figure 3.7.

Enter the label, value, or formula you want to search for in the Find What text box, mark the appropriate option buttons and check box to specify the parameters of your search, and then select OK to begin.

If Excel finds an entry that matches your search parameters, it moves the cell selector to that cell. To resume searching, press F7.

## THE REPLACE COMMAND

When you choose the Replace command, Excel displays the dialog box shown in Figure 3.8.

**FIGURE 3.7:**
The Find dialog box.

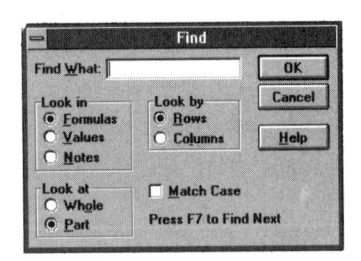

**FIGURE 3.8:**
The Replace dialog box.

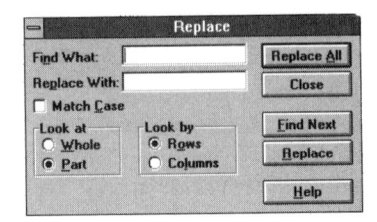

*Checking Your Spelling*

Enter the item you want to find, and also the label, value, or formula you want to replace it with. Mark the option buttons and check box as appropriate.

Use the Replace All button, and Excel will automatically find and replace all the items you've designated. The Find Next and Replace buttons allow you to replace found entries on an individual basis. The Close button stops the operation.

> **TIP** *With large or complex worksheets, you can streamline your find and replace efforts by first selecting the specific range you want to search. If you don't do this, Excel searches your entire worksheet.*

# CHECKING YOUR SPELLING

Excel lets you check the spelling of a selected word, a selected range, or all the words on your worksheet. Choose the Spelling command from the Options menu to display the Spelling dialog box shown in Figure 3.9.

> **NOTE** *When you first use the Spelling command, Excel asks your permission to create a dictionary file named CUSTOM.DIC. This file is used to store any words you add.*

Excel finds and displays words that are not in its dictionary. If you select the Suggest button, Excel creates a list of suggestions. Checking the Always Suggest box tells Excel to make suggestions automatically.

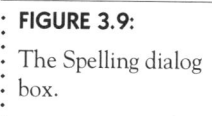

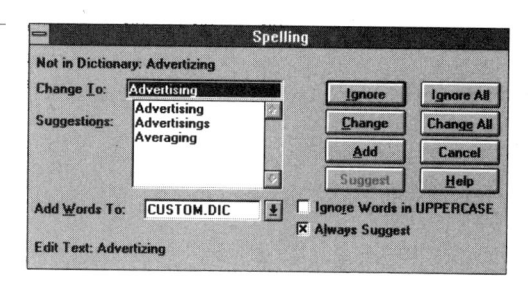

**FIGURE 3.9:**

The Spelling dialog box.

**35**

*Building a Framework of Editing Skills*
**LESSON 3**

- If the spelling is correct, and you don't expect the word to occur outside the current document, select the Ignore or Ignore All button. Excel ignores words in all uppercase if you check the Ignore Words in UPPERCASE box. If you expect the word to occur frequently, select the Add button, and Excel will add it to your personal dictionary (CUSTOM.DIC) or another dictionary listed in the Add Words To box.

- If the spelling really is incorrect, type the correct spelling in the Change To text box or select one of Excel's suggestions, and then select the Change or Change All buttons.

To stop the spell-checking process, select the Cancel button. When the checking operation is allowed to run, the Cancel button changes to the Close button. Select the Close button when you're finished checking your spelling.

# LOOKING AHEAD

Lesson 3 has provided you with a quick overview of Excel's basic editing features. For more information on the subjects introduced in this lesson, see the following topics in the Reference section of this book.

Cell Characteristics

Clearing Data

Consolidating Data

Outlining Worksheet Data

Pasting Link Formulas

Pasting Data from the Clipboard

Repeating the Last Command

Replacing Cell Data

Series Values

Lesson 4 shows you how to enhance your worksheets with a formidable array of formatting tools. If you plan to take a break at this point, be sure to save your worksheet before you exit the program.

# 4

# ENHANCING YOUR WORK WITH FORMATTING

**INTRODUCING**

*Excel's AutoFormat command*
*Aligning labels and values*
*Assigning formats to numbers*
*Changing font styles and sizes*
*Creating borders and shaded cells*
*Modifying column and row size*

With proper formatting, your worksheets are easier to read and more visually attractive. This lesson puts you on the fast track to enhancing your work with Excel's formatting features. If you haven't already done so, start Excel and retrieve your BUDGET.XLS worksheet if you want to practice this lesson's techniques on-line.

*Enhancing Your Work with Formatting*
**LESSON 4**

# USING THE AUTOFORMAT COMMAND

Excel's AutoFormat feature performs many standard formatting tasks in a single operation: it sets fonts, alignment of labels, column width and row height, and numeric and date/time formats (collectively known as pictures), and it can add borders and rules. Like most of Excel's basic features, Autoformat can be accessed with a menu command or by selecting it from the toolbar.

To demonstrate the AutoFormat command, edit the budgeting worksheet so it looks like the one shown in Figure 4.1. Insert two rows at the top of the budgeting worksheet. Delete one of the rows between the budgeting categories and the formulas. Then enter the label **Monthly Expense Budget** in cell A1 and the labels **Jan**, **Feb**, and **Mar** in C2, D2, and E2, respectively. If you have questions about inserting rows or entering labels, refer to Lessons 1 and 3.

To use the AutoFormat command to add formatting to a worksheet like the one shown in Figure 4.1, you would follow these steps:

1. Select the worksheet range you want to format. In Figure 4.1, this range is A1:E9.

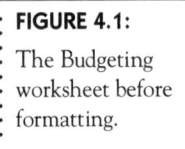

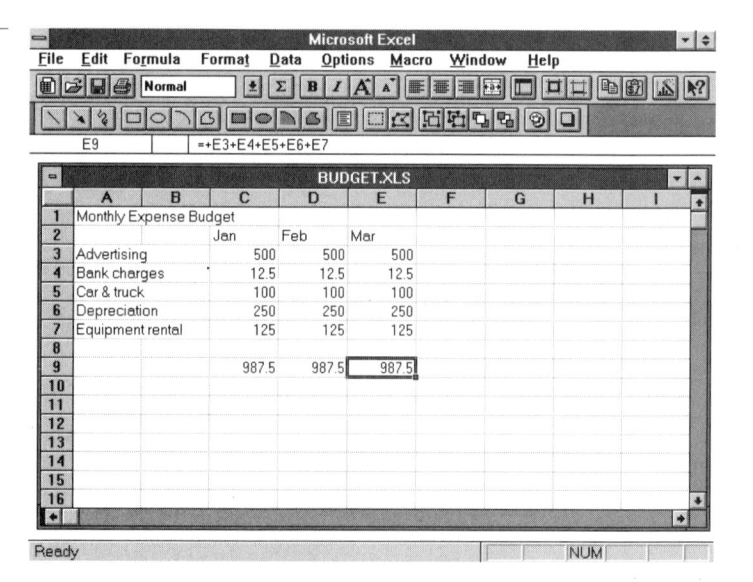

**FIGURE 4.1:**

The Budgeting worksheet before formatting.

38

*Using the AutoFormat Command*

2. Choose AutoFormat from the Format menu. Excel displays the dialog box shown in Figure 4.2.

3. Choose one of Excel's AutoFormats from the Table Format list. You can observe its effect in the Sample box.

4. To apply an AutoFormat to your selected worksheet range, select the OK button. Figure 4.3 shows the budgeting worksheet after the first automatic formatting option, Classic 1, is applied.

Take a moment to review Figure 4.3. It illustrates many of the formatting options available for Excel worksheets, including lines, font setting, and alignment.

5. Repeat the steps above to try out different formats. Then, after you've reviewed their effects on the worksheet, choose the Undo command to

**FIGURE 4.2:**
The AutoFormat dialog box.

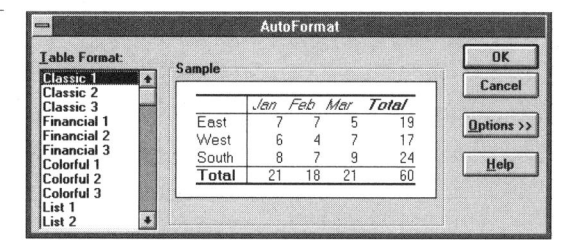

**FIGURE 4.3:**
The budgeting worksheet after the automatic formatting.

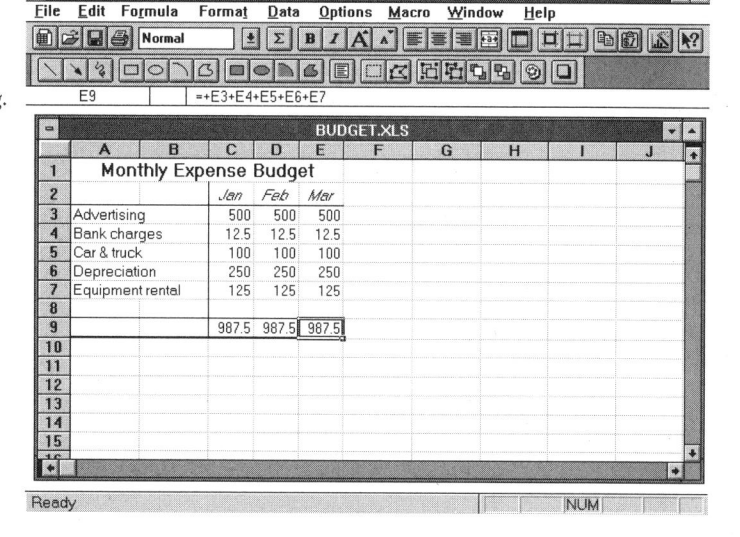

*Enhancing Your Work with Formatting*
**LESSON 4**

remove the formatting. This way, we can continue to use the budgeting worksheet to illustrate manual formatting options.

The AutoFormat tool on the toolbar applies either a currently selected format or the default Classic 1 format to a selected range.

## SELECTIVE AUTOFORMATTING

The Options button on the AutoFormat dialog box lets you apply formatting features selectively. Again, the best way to learn about these features is to experiment with them. Doing so will help you decide which of Excel's settings you can accept, and which ones you will need to set manually.

## WORKING WITH MANUAL FORMATTING

As you learn to create more complex and specialized worksheets, your formatting efforts require similar treatment. The following sections detail each of Excel's formatting features. Like the AutoFormat command, each feature can usually be accessed from a menu as well as the toolbar.

## ALIGNING LABELS AND VALUES

Excel normally aligns values against the right edge of a cell and labels against the left edge. You can override these default alignments by using the Left Align, Center, Right Align, and Center Across Selection tools on the tool bar. Let's center the label in cell A1 across the range A1:E1 on your Budget.XLS worksheet. First select the range A1:E1, and then select the Center Across Selection tool. Figure 4.4 shows your worksheet after this alignment. The Center tool only centers a label or value in a single cell.

You can access a more sophisticated array of alignment features by choosing the Alignment command from the Format or Shortcuts menu. Excel displays the Alignment dialog box shown in Figure 4.5.

Among the Horizontal alignment options, General is the default (values right-aligned, labels left-aligned). Left, Center, and Right alignment applies to all entries regardless of type. Center Across Selection requires you to select all or part

**40**

*Working with Manual Formatting*

**FIGURE 4.4:**

The label centered across range A1:E1.

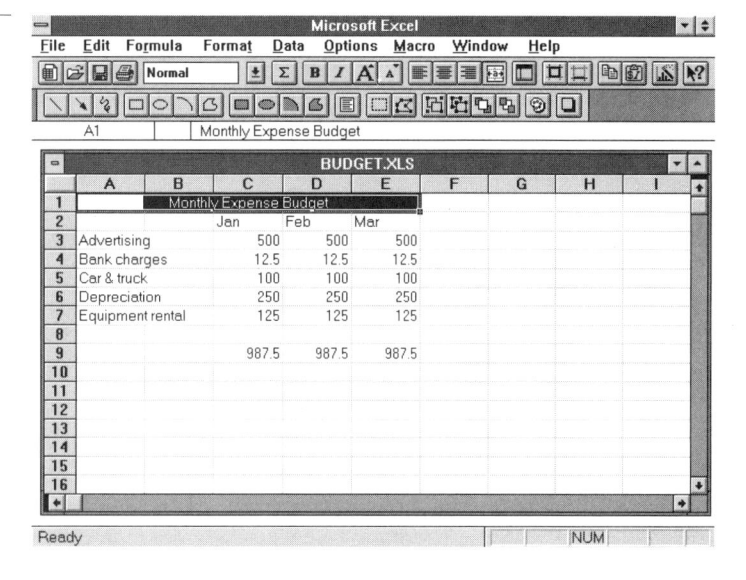

**FIGURE 4.5:**

The Alignment dialog box.

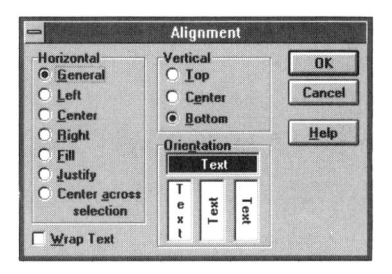

of a row. Fill repeats a label or value as many times as it will fit in a cell. If there are empty cells to the right of a cell and you've assigned them the Fill alignment, they're also filled. Justify aligns your text both left and right when the Wrap Text box is checked.

The Vertical option buttons allow you to align your entry at the top, center, or bottom of a cell. The default setting is Bottom, and you won't need to change it unless you've also changed the row height. The Orientation buttons rotate selected labels and values as shown.

**WARNING**

*You may need to adjust row height in your selected range to accommodate rotated text. This topic is covered later in this lesson.*

**41**

*Enhancing Your Work with Formatting*
**LESSON 4**

## ASSIGNING FORMATS TO NUMBERS

[Normal] You can assign numeric formats such as dollar signs, percentage symbols, and commas by using the Number command or the toolbar's Style box. To format the values in the budgeting worksheet, you would follow these steps:

1. Select the worksheet range that holds the values by clicking on cell C3 and dragging the mouse to cell E9.

2. Choose Format (or Shortcuts) ➤ Number to display the Number Format ialog box shown in Figure 4.6. The Category box shows the seven available formats, with All as the default setting. The Format Code demonstrate the appearance of options. General is the default setting (no commas, no dollar sign, one decimal place). For the other codes, the pound sign (#) stands for a digit. The Sample text box shows how the value in the active cell appears when a format code is applied.

> *You can also use the Code text box to create custom formatting codes. See* **Mastering Excel 4 for Windows,** *by Carl Townsend (SYBEX, 1992) for details.*

3. Scroll through the list and choose the $#,##0_);($#,###0) code.

4. Select the OK button. Figure 4.7 shows the result.

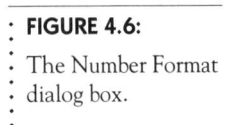

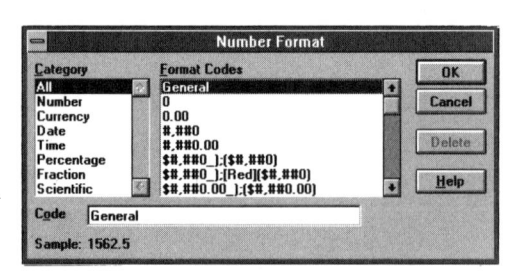

**FIGURE 4.6:**
The Number Format dialog box.

*Working with Manual Formatting*

**FIGURE 4.7:**
Your worksheet with formatted numbers.

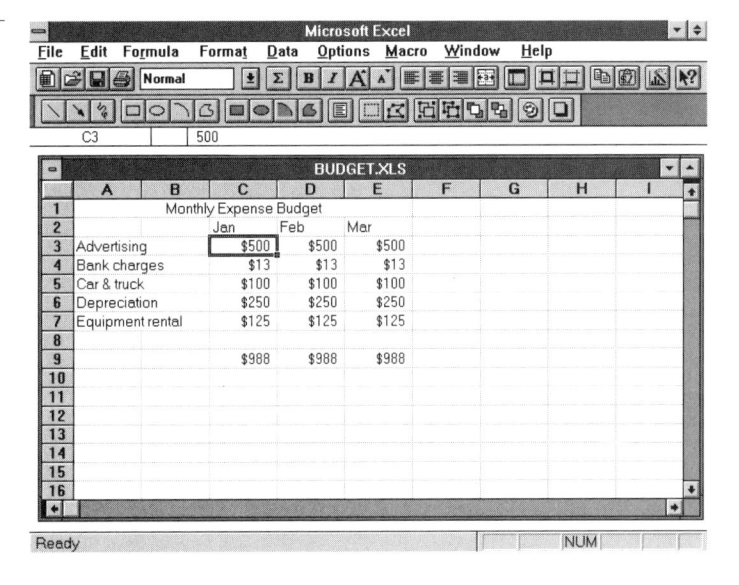

*The fastest way to format numbers is with the Style box on the toolbar. The default setting is Normal, but when you activate the drop down list box, six additional formats are displayed.*

Take a few minutes to experiment with the various formatting options we've covered so far. Remember, you can use the Undo command to undo your last action. Be sure to retain a version of your worksheet similar to the one shown in Figure 4.7. We'll be using this worksheet for later exercises.

## CHANGING FONT STYLES AND SIZES

Excel offers a wide variety of choices for selecting the best font styles and sizes for your worksheet. There are four font tools on Excel's tool bar for making quick changes to bold or italic text, and to larger or smaller point sizes.

Select the label in range A1:E1, and then the Bold and Italic tools. Figure 4.8 shows how your worksheet should look when you're done.

The Fonts command lets you select a full array of font characteristics including different type styles, strikeouts and underlines, and a variety of colors. Choose Format (or Shortcuts) ➤ Font to display the Font dialog box shown in Figure 4.9.

**43**

*Enhancing Your Work with Formatting*
**LESSON 4**

You select type styles from the Font list box. Fonts marked with a TT icon are True-Type fonts, which are available only in Windows 3.1 and can be matched exactly even by many dot-matrix printers. Fonts built into your printer have a printer icon

**FIGURE 4.8:**

Your worksheet with bold and italic labels.

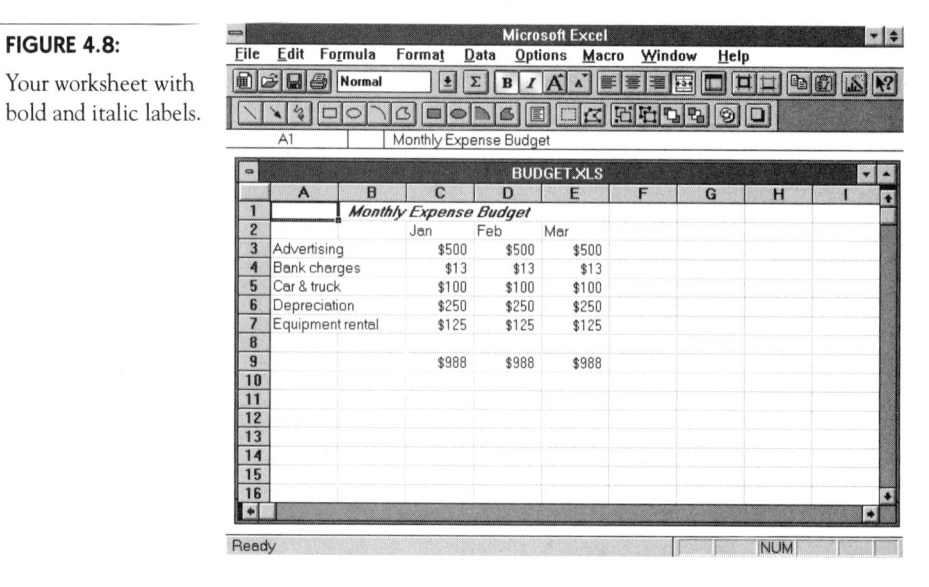

**FIGURE 4.9:**

The Font dialog box.

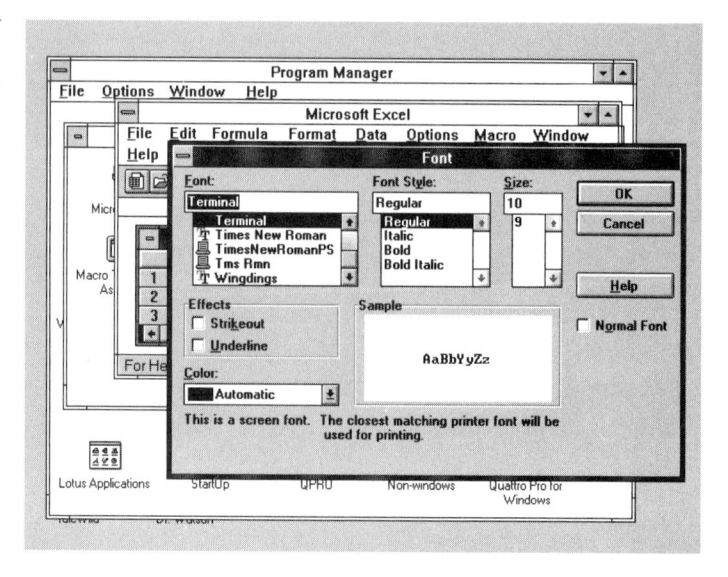

44

next to them. The Font Style box lets you choose Regular, Italic, Bold, or Bold Italic. To change point sizes, use the Size list box.

> *Points are used to measure font sizes. A point is 1/72 inch. Common point sizes include 8, 10, 12, 14, 18, 24.*

Special effects, such as Strikeout and Underline, are activated by their check boxes. Colors other than Automatic, which is black, can be selected from the Color drop-down list box. The Sample text box illustrates the current font selection, and the Normal Font check box resets the font style to regular.

> *As noted on the Font dialog box, Excel prints your worksheet with the closest matching printer font if your printer won't support your font selection. Unless you're using a TrueType font, what you see on your screen may not be what you get on your printed documents. In Windows, see the Help screens for the Control Panel for instructions on installing and using fonts.*

## CREATING BORDERS AND SHADED CELLS

One of Excel's niftier formatting features allows you to create lines and shading that help organize, clarify, and emphasize the information on your worksheet. To add rules and shading, use the Border dialog box:

1. Choose Format (or Shortcuts) ➤ Border to display the dialog box shown in Figure 4.10.

2. Select one of the Border option buttons to designate the line location on your selected worksheet range.

3. Select one of the Style buttons to select a variety of thicknesses, dashed, or double line styles.

    To select a color other than black, activate the color list box.

4. To shade the cells in your selected range, mark the Shade check box.

*Enhancing Your Work with Formatting*
**LESSON 4**

**FIGURE 4.10:**
The Border dialog box.

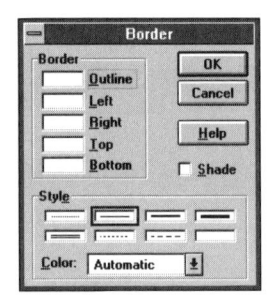

> **NOTE:** To change Excel's default shading style and color, choose Format (or Shortcuts) ➤ Patterns to display the Patterns dialog box.

For quicker formatting, Excel provides two line-drawing tools on the toolbar. The Draw Box tool creates an outside border around a selected worksheet range, and the Draw Line tool draws a line along the bottom edge of a selected range.

## MODIFYING COLUMN AND ROW SIZE

As you reformat the labels and values in your worksheet, you may need to modify the standard column and row sizes to accommodate your formatting changes. The Row Height and ColumnWidth commands allow you to make precise adjustments to these dimensions, and also hide and unhide selected columns or rows.

> **TIP:** The easiest way to modify a column or row dimension is to point to the right or bottom edge of the border for the column or row you want to change. When the mouse pointer changes to a two-sided arrow, hold down the left mouse button and drag the edge of the column or row to create the desired dimension.

Choose the Row Height command from the Format menu to display the dialog box shown in Figure 4.11.

To change the height of a selected row, enter the desired height in points. Mark the Standard Height check box to reset the 12.75 point default. Use the Hide and Unhide buttons to hide or redisplay a selected row. To display a row you've hidden, select a range that includes the rows above and below the hidden row before selecting Unhide.

The Column Width command on the Format menu displays the dialog box in Figure 4.12.

Enter the desired column width in characters, or select the Best Fit button for automatic adjustment to the widest label or value. Mark the Use Standard Width box to reset the default to 8.43 characters. The Hide and Unhide buttons let you hide or redisplay a column. To unhide a column, select the range of columns including those to the left and right of the hidden column before selecting Unhide.

**FIGURE 4.11:**
The Row Height dialog box.

**FIGURE 4.12:**
The Column Width dialog box.

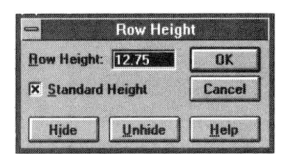

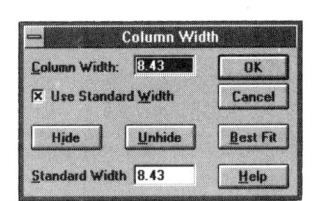

# LOOKING AHEAD

Lesson 4 has demonstrated some basic tools for making your worksheets easier to read and more visually attractive. For more information on the subjects introduced in this lesson, consult the following Reference entries:

    Color Palette

    Drawing Features

    Formatting

    Sorting Worksheet Data

Lesson 5 provides some valuable insights and practical information on printing and managing your files. If you plan to take a break at this point, be sure to save your worksheet before you exit the program.

# 5

# Printing and Managing Your Files

**INTRODUCING**

*Printing with Excel*

*The Page Setup and Print Preview commands*

*The Options menu printing commands*

*Managing multiple files in memory*

*Erasing files*

*Exporting and importing files*

Printing with Excel is faster and easier than with most other popular spreadsheet programs. Excel also has several unique and convenient file management features that allow you to work with more than one file at a time, and import or export a variety of other types of document files. Let's take a quick look at these functions. If you haven't already done so, start Excel and retrieve your BUDGET.XLS worksheet if you want to work on-line.

*Printing and Managing Your Files*
**LESSON 5**

If you haven't already set up your printer with Windows, or if there are any problems that would prevent you from trying out these procedures, consult your Windows documentation.

# PRINTING WITH EXCEL

To print your BUDGET.XLS worksheet, follow these steps:

1. Choose the Print command from the File menu. Excel displays the Print dialog box, shown in Figure 5.1.

2. To print only part of the worksheet, select Pages in the Print Range area and then enter the page number range in the From and To text boxes.

3. Use the Print Quality drop-down list box to select the printer resolution. Higher print quality settings, of course, look crisper and are more legible but they take more time to print. Lower print quality settings, on the other hand, print more quickly but don't look as nice.

4. Use the Copies text box to specify how many copies of the worksheet should be printed.

5. Select OK, and Excel begins printing the worksheet.

> *The Print dialog box also lets you create a print file, collate printed copies, and print just your worksheet, cell notes only, or both. Refer to the on-line help program for more information on these print options.*

**FIGURE 5.1:**

The Print dialog box.

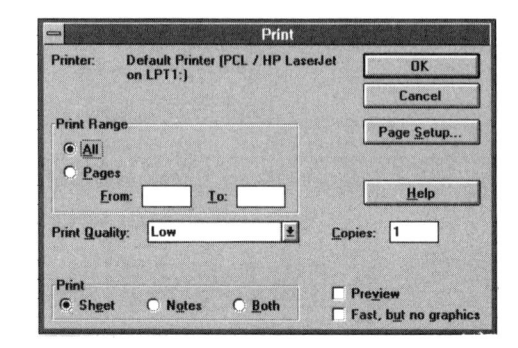

*Printing with Excel*

When you don't need to change the settings in the Print dialog box, you can print your worksheet at any time by selecting the Print tool on the toolbar.

## SETTING UP PAGES

The Page Setup dialog box, shown in Figure 5.2, gives you precise control over how your worksheet will be printed. Select the Setup button on the Print dialog box or choose File ➤ Page Setup to display the dialog box.

The Orientation option buttons allow you to select either the standard portrait or a horizontal landscape orientation for your printed worksheet pages. You can choose a paper size appropriate for your printer by activating the Paper Size list box. The Margins text boxes let you enter your preferences in inches, and the Center check boxes center your printed worksheet horizontally or vertically between your chosen margins.

Check the Row & Column Headings box to print the column letter and row number borders, and the Cell Gridlines box to print gridlines between worksheet cells. Use the Black & White Cells check box to print colored cells in black and white, and the Start Page No.'s At text box to choose and enter a number for the first page of your printed worksheet.

To print and break your worksheet pages by columns, mark the Down, then Over option button. To print and break your worksheet pages by rows, mark the Over, then Down button. The Scaling option buttons and text boxes let you size your worksheet by a specified percentage or to fit a specific number of pages.

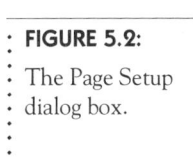

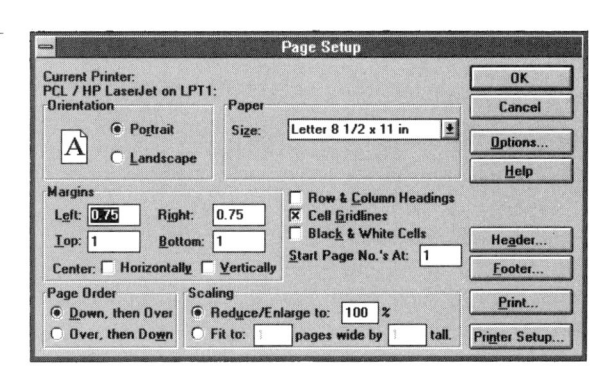

**FIGURE 5.2:**
The Page Setup dialog box.

**51**

*Printing and Managing Your Files*
**LESSON 5**

> *When the active document is a chart, the Page Setup dialog box includes the Chart Size option buttons. These buttons control chart printing. Refer to Lesson 6 for more information on Excel's charting features.*

The Page Setup dialog box also has several command buttons. The Options button displays a dialog box for choosing the options supported by your active printer. The Header and Footer buttons display dialog boxes for adding or changing these items at the top and bottom margins on each of your printed pages. The Print button prints your worksheet, and the Printer Setup button displays a dialog box for changing the active printer.

> *As you learn about Excel's wide variety of printing and page setup options, use your BUDGET.XLS worksheet to experiment with them and view the printed results. We'll be creating other sample worksheets in subsequent lessons so you needn't retain a saved version of BUDGET.XLS.*

## THE PRINT PREVIEW COMMAND

The Print Preview command lets you see what a printed worksheet will look like before you print it. Using the Print Preview command, for example, you can see how many pages it takes to print a worksheet and how each of the printed pages will look.

To illustrate how the command works using the BUDGET.XLS worksheet, simply choose File ➤ Print Preview or select Preview from the Print dialog box. Excel displays a print preview of your BUDGET.XLS worksheet as shown in Figure 5.3. To make it easier to view the content of our sample worksheet, the Cell Gridlines check box on the Page Setup dialog box has been left unmarked.

The Print Preview Window has seven command buttons. Next and Previous allow you to page back and forth through multi-page worksheet files. The Zoom button enlarges the previewed page to fill the window as in Figure 5.4.

**52**

*Printing with Excel*

**FIGURE 5.3:**

The Print Preview window.

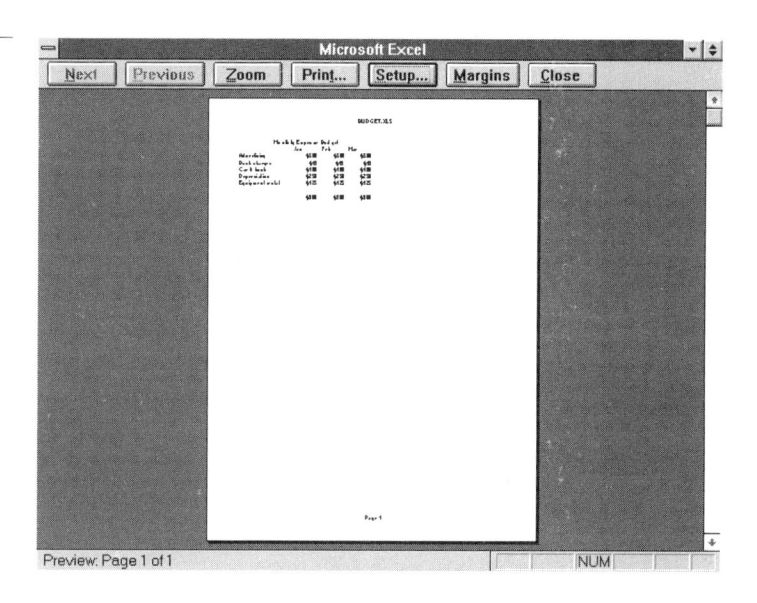

**FIGURE 5.4:**

The Print Preview window with Zoom selected.

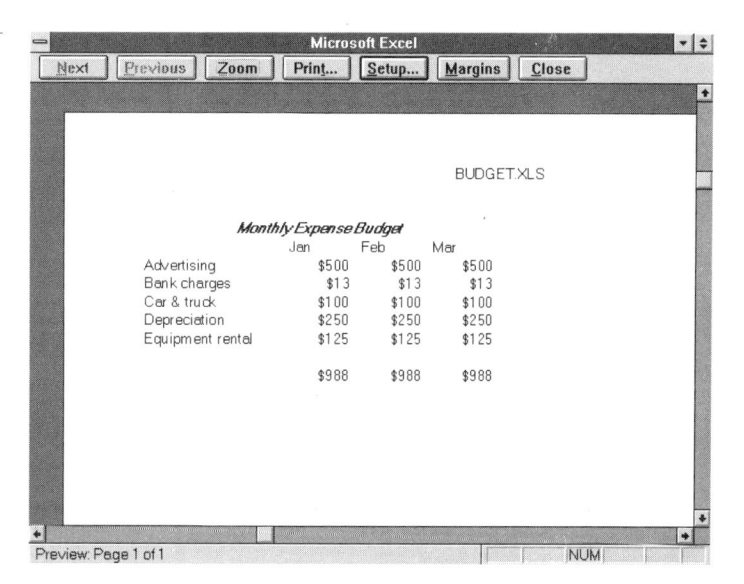

*Printing and Managing Your Files*
**LESSON 5**

> **TIP** *If you're using a mouse, selecting the Zoom button changes your mouse pointer to a magnifying glass symbol. You can zoom in on specific portions of your worksheet by pointing the magnifying glass symbol and clicking the left mouse button.*

The Print button prints your worksheet, Setup displays the Page Setup dialog box, and the Margins button displays the dashed margin lines shown in Figure 5.5. You can change your page margins by moving these lines with your mouse.

To remove the Print Preview Window, select the Close button.

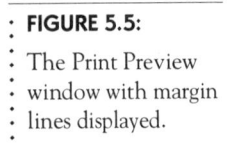

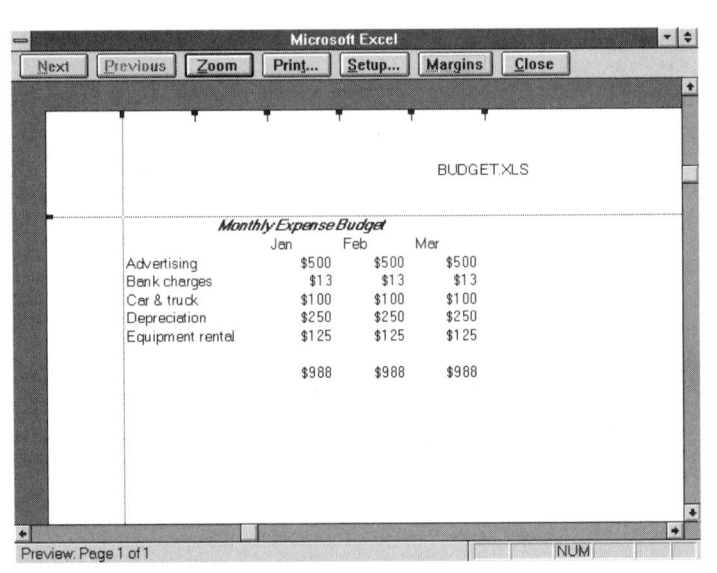

**FIGURE 5.5:**
The Print Preview window with margin lines displayed.

## OPTIONS MENU PRINT COMMANDS

When you activate Excel's Options menu, as shown in Figure 5.6, three additional printing options become available.

***Set Print Area***  To set a specific area of your worksheet for printing, take the following steps:

1. Select the range you want printed.
2. Choose Options ➤ Set Print Area.

*Printing with Excel*

Excel draws dashed lines along the print area's borders, and when you use the File menu's Print command, Excel prints only the range you set as the print area. To change the print area, select a new worksheet range, and then reactivate the Set Print Area command.

**FIGURE 5.6:**
The Options menu print commands.

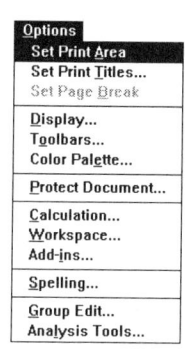

> *To remove the set print area and make your entire worksheet available for printing, you can use the Define Name command on the Formula menu. Refer to the Range entry for more information on the Define Name command.*

***Set Print Titles*** When working with large worksheets that need more than one page for printing, you may want to designate a particular row or column to appear as a title on each printed page of your worksheet. Choose Options ➤ Set Print Titles to display the dialog box shown in Figure 5.7.

Enter the row or column range address you want to use in the appropriate text box. You don't need to enter all the letters and numbers in the range definition, but you should make your definition absolute. To set row 1 as a horizontal print title, enter the definition $1:$1. To set column A as a vertical print title, enter the definition $A:$A.

**FIGURE 5.7:**
The Set Print Titles dialog box.

**55**

*Printing and Managing Your Files*
**LESSON 5**

> *TIP*
>
> *The fastest way to set print titles is to first select a row or column by clicking on its number or letter in the row or column border, and then choosing the Set Print Titles command. To select a row and column for both horizontal and vertical print titles, first select the row, and then select the column while holding down the Ctrl key.*

***Set Page Break*** Excel automatically breaks pages as they are normally filled in printing. To force Excel to set a page break at a specific location on your worksheet, first select the column or row that follows the place you want the break, and then choose Options ➤ Set Page Break. To remove a page break, select the column or row that follows the break, and then choose Options ➤ Remove Page Break.

# MANAGING YOUR FILES WITH EXCEL

Excel lets you work with more than one worksheet file at a time, and export and import files to and from other applications. All of these capabilities are available through the File menu. Let's briefly discuss each of them.

## HANDLING MULTIPLE FILES

When you start Excel, an empty worksheet file named SHEET1.XLS is automatically opened. To open an existing worksheet file, use File ➤ Open as described in Lesson 2.

To open additional blank worksheets, follow these steps:

**1.** Choose File ➤ New. Excel displays the dialog box shown in Figure 5.8.

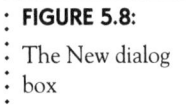

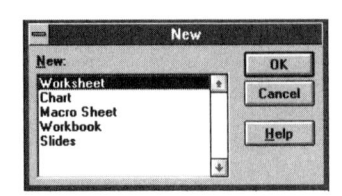

**FIGURE 5.8:**
The New dialog box

## Managing Your Files with Excel

2. Select the file type from the list box: Worksheet to open a new, blank worksheet, Chart to open a new, blank chart document, Macro Sheet to open a new, blank macro sheet, Workbook to open a new, blank workbook, or Slides to open a new, blank slide show file.

If you want to open a new, blank worksheet file, you can also choose the New worksheet tool on the toolbar.

3. Select OK and Excel opens a new blank file of the type you specified.

Each of your open files is displayed in a separate document window, and each window is listed as an option on Excel's Window menu. To activate a window, select it from the Window menu. To remove an active window, choose the File menu's Close command. If your worksheet has been changed and isn't flagged as read-only (see Security in the Reference), Excel asks whether to save your changes before closing.

> *To close all your open worksheet files, press and hold the Shift key while activating the File menu. Excel replaces the File menu's Close command with the Close All command.*

## DELETING FILES

To erase Excel files you no longer need, follow these steps:

1. Choose File ➤ Delete to display the dialog box shown in Figure 5.9.
2. Use the Drives list box to indicate the disk drive from which to delete the file.

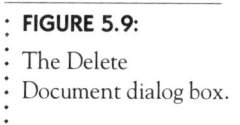

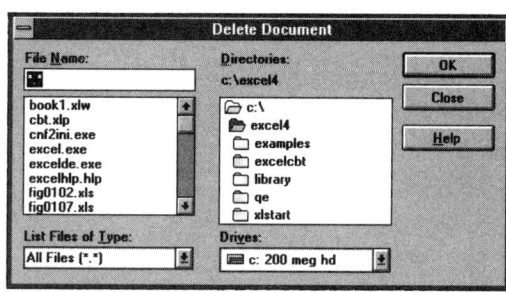

**FIGURE 5.9:**
The Delete Document dialog box.

**57**

*Printing and Managing Your Files*
**LESSON 5**

3. Use the Directory list box to indicate the directory from which to delete the file.
4. Select the file from the File Name list or enter its name in the text box.
5. When the dialog box is complete, select OK to delete the file.

## EXPORTING AND IMPORTING

To create a worksheet file you can export to another application, choose the File menu's Save As command to display the File Save As dialog box. Activate the Save File as Type list, shown in Figure 5.10, and select the type of file you want to create.

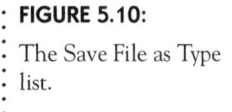

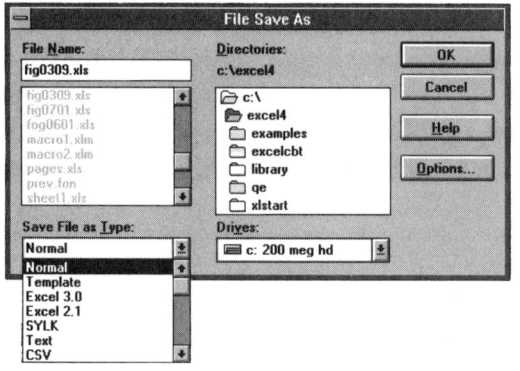

**FIGURE 5.10:**
The Save File as Type list.

> *There are almost two dozen export file formats available for different kinds of Excel files. SYLK files are standard ASCII=formatted database files that let you easily exchange spreadsheets between different operating systems, such as DOS and Macintosh, with formats and formulas intact. For more information on choosing the correct export file types, refer to your Excel documentation.*

To retrieve a worksheet file originally created by another application, choose the Open command from the File menu to display the File Open dialog box. Activate the List Files of Type list, shown in Figure 5.11, and select the type of file you want to retrieve or import.

**FIGURE 5.11:**

The List Files of Type list.

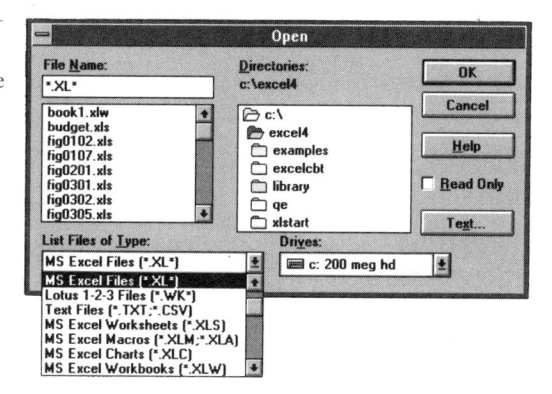

> *If you're attempting to import a text file, you can let Excel apply a default set of assumptions to the file or you can select the Text command button on the File Open dialog box. Excel displays a Text File Options dialog box that lets you describe the text file's column delimiters and the system that created the file. For more information on this feature, see your Excel documentation.*

# LOOKING AHEAD

This lesson has taught you the basic printing and file management skills you need to get the most from Excel in the shortest period of time. For more information on the subjects introduced in this lesson, see the following topics in the Reference section of this book:

- Annotating Cells
- Document Windows
- Importing and Exporting Data
- Linking Files
- Printing

The next lesson advances your level of skill even further, with a thorough discussion of Excel's powerful charting features.

# 6

# Presenting Your Data with Charts

**INTRODUCTING**

*Creating charts with the ChartWizard*

*Formatting with the Chart toolbar*

*Saving charts as independent files*

*Printing charts as separate items*

After arranging your information in the rows and columns of a worksheet, you can use Excel's charting features to represent your worksheet data graphically. Charts can add visual impact to your document. By highlighting trends or changes, they can also help you present information more effectively.

*Presenting Your Data with Charts*
**LESSON 6**

# CREATING AND WORKING WITH CHARTS

Excel lets you create a full range of charts including line charts, area charts, bar and column charts, and pie charts. In this lesson you'll be creating a new worksheet to use as a sample document. If you have the BUDGET.XLS worksheet open on your screen, use the File menu's Close command to remove it, and then the New command or the toolbar's New Worksheet tool to open a blank worksheet. If you haven't already done so, start Excel and a blank worksheet document is automatically displayed.

## USING THE CHARTWIZARD

The easiest and most direct way to convert your worksheets to charts is with Excel's ChartWizard. Let's create a sample worksheet, and then explore ChartWizard step-by-step.

To follow along on-line, you can build the sample worksheet shown in Figure 6.1. It represents five years of sales revenue data for three fictitious companies: Acme, National, and Republic. When you've entered your data, use the File menu's Save As command to name your document SALES.XLS.

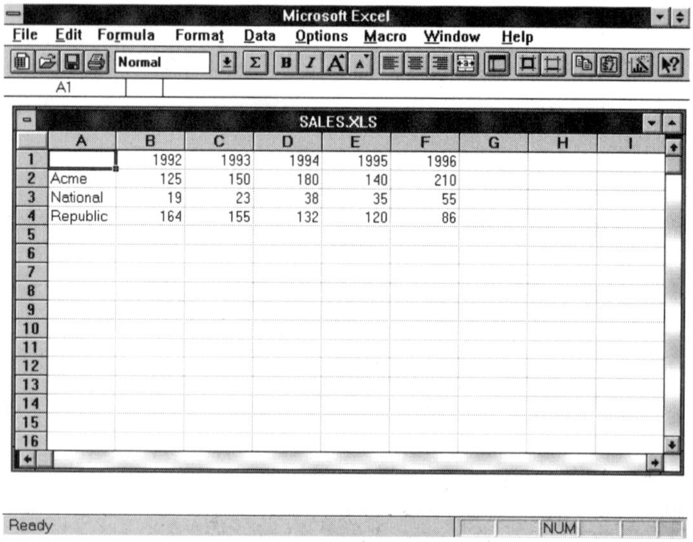

**FIGURE 6.1:**
A sample worksheet suitable for charting.

*Creating and Working with Charts*

> To chart worksheet data, you need to understand some terminology. A **data series** is a set of one or more related numeric values. In our sample SALES.XLS worksheet, each set of sales figures represents a different data series. The individual bits of data that make up a data series are called **data points.** The data series for Acme consists of five revenue figures, for example, so it has five data points. **Categories** represent the other view of the chart data; usually, categories are time periods. For example, Figure 6.1 provides sales revenue for the years, or categories, 1992, 1993, 1994, 1995, and 1996. A **time-series** data comparison is one where the categories are time periods.

The ChartWizard converts your worksheet data to charts in five simple steps. Dialog boxes appear at each step to guide you through the process.

To use the ChartWizard, follow these steps:

1. Select the worksheet range you want to chart. Include any row or column headings in your selection. Select range A1:F4 on your sample worksheet.

2. Select the ChartWizard tool from the toolbar. Excel changes your mouse pointer to a cross-hair.

3. Point the cross-hair to the upper-left corner of the area where you want your chart placed. Holding down the left mouse button, drag the cross-hair to the point where you want the lower-right corner of your chart. Excel draws a box to show the placement of your chart, and displays the first of five Chart-Wizard dialog boxes (Figure 6.2). This dialog box lets you select a new range on your worksheet or enter a new range definition in the text box.

4. To continue, select the Next button. Excel displays the second Chart-Wizard dialog box (Figure 6.3), showing the basic chart types available in Excel.

5. To follow this example, you would select Line chart and then Next. Excel displays the third ChartWizard dialog box, shown in Figure 6.4, which offers various formats for the line chart.

6. Select the format you want (format 1, if you're following along on-line) by pointing to it, and select the Next button to continue. Excel displays the fourth ChartWizard dialog box, with your sample Line chart, as shown in Figure 6.5.

**63**

*Presenting Your Data with Charts*
**LESSON 6**

**FIGURE 6.2:**

The ChartWizard range selection dialog box.

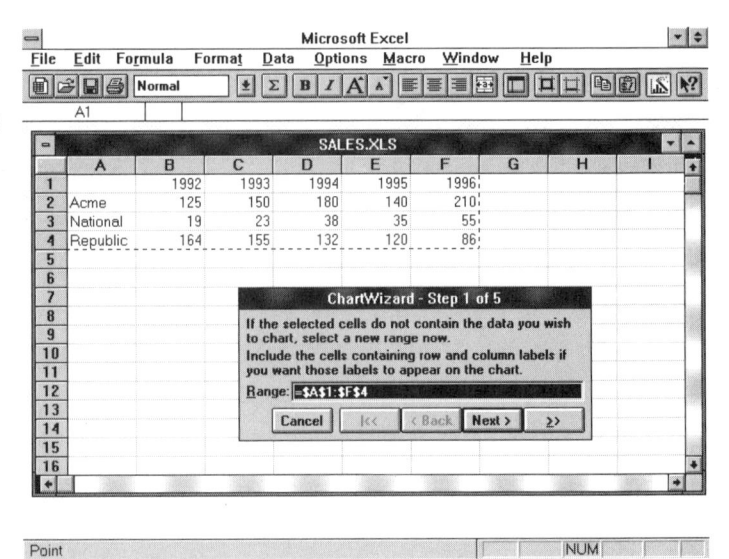

**FIGURE 6.3:**

The ChartWizard chart selection dialog box.

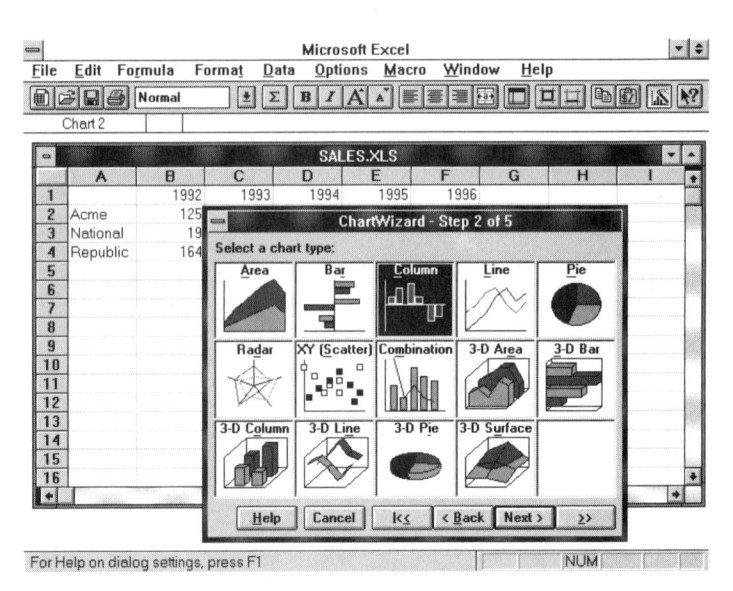

**64**

*Creating and Working with Charts*

**FIGURE 6.4:**

The ChartWizard format selection dialog box.

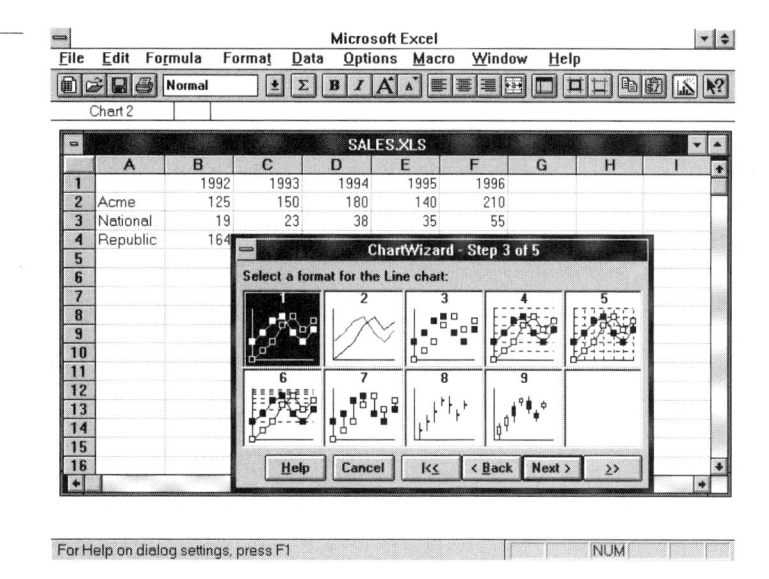

**FIGURE 6.5:**

The ChartWizard rows and columns dialog box.

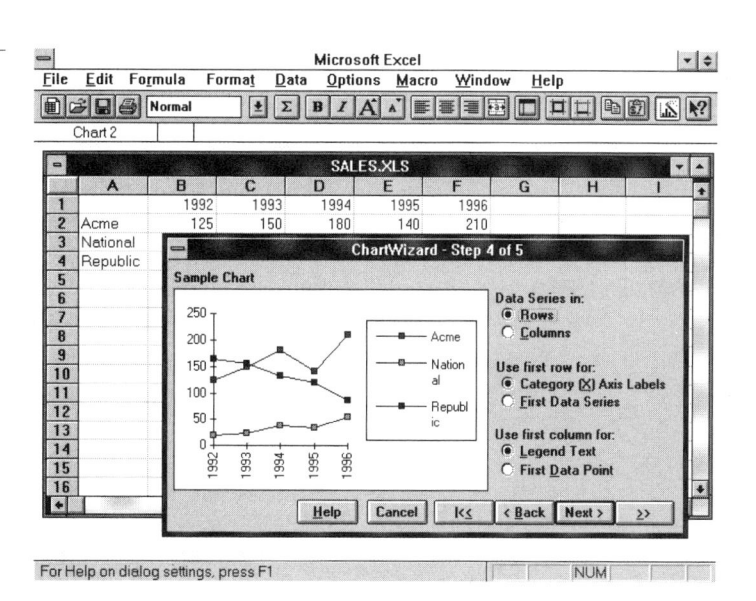

**65**

*Presenting Your Data with Charts*
**LESSON 6**

7. The ChartWizard makes certain assumptions about your worksheet and how it should be plotted. Use the option buttons in this dialog box if you need to change any assumptions:

   - If the data series occupy columns in your worksheet rather than the usual rows, choose Colunms under Data Series.
   - If the first row of your worksheet contains data rather than labels, choose First Data Series under Use First Row For.
   - If the first column of your worksheet contains data rather than labels, choose First Data Point under Use First Column For.

   In our example, we can leave the default settings shown in Figure 6.5.

8. Select the Next command button to display the fifth and final ChartWizard dialog box, shown in Figure 6.6.

9. If you don't want the ChartWizard to include a legend on your chart, mark the No button.

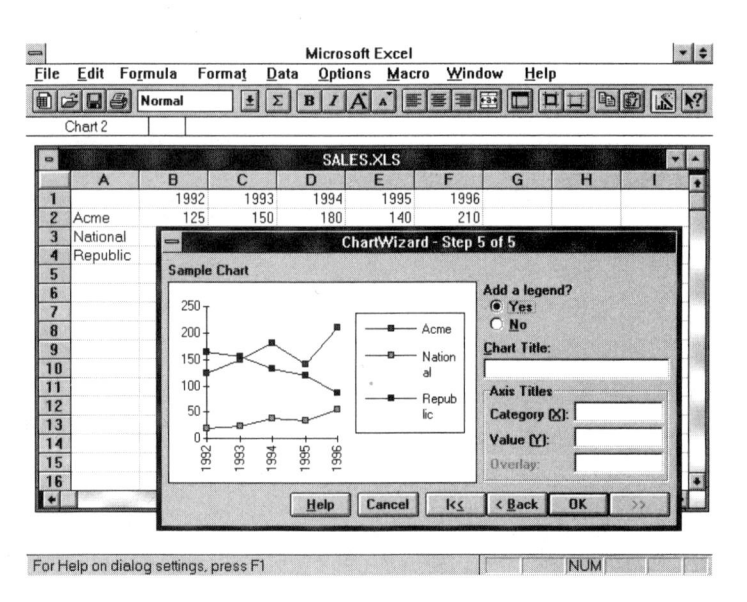

**FIGURE 6.6:**
The ChartWizard legends and titles dialog box.

*Creating and Working with Charts*

> **NOTE** *If the first column or row of a data series includes descriptive text, like the Acme, National, and Republic labels in our sample worksheet, the ChartWizard uses this text in the legend. Otherwise, the first data series is described as Series 1, the second as Series 2, and so on.*

**10.** Use the Chart Title text box to give the chart a title. For this example, you would enter the chart title "Five-Year Revenue Comparison." Use the Axis Titles Category and Axis Titles Value text boxes if you want to give the horizontal and vertical axes titles. For this example, enter the Category axis title as "Years" and the Value axis title as "Sales." To complete the process, select OK. Excel places the completed chart on your worksheet as shown in Figure 6.7.

**FIGURE 6.7:**
Your completed Line chart.

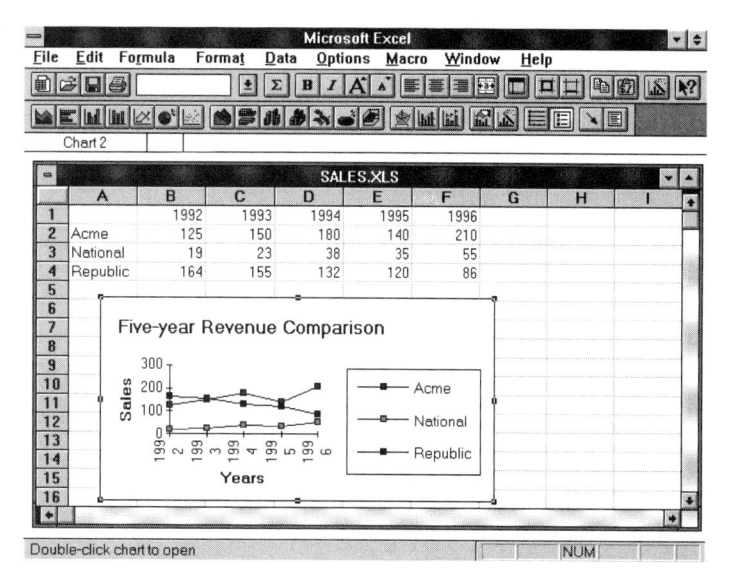

**67**

*Presenting Your Data with Charts*
**LESSON 6**

> **TIP**
> 
> *You can use your mouse to move and resize a chart. To move a chart, place the mouse pointer anywhere inside the chart and, holding down the left mouse button, drag it to the new location. To resize your chart, first select the chart by clicking it. Then place the mouse pointer on one of the small square chart handles that appear on the corners and along each side of the chart and, holding down the left mouse button, drag it until you've achieved the correct size and shape. This is a quick and effective way to adjust the chart size to accommodate the length of chart titles and labels.*

## WORKING WITH THE CHART TOOLBAR

Once you've created a chart and placed it on your worksheet, Excel adds the Chart toolbar below your application window, as shown in Figure 6.7. You can use the various Chart tools to reformat and customize your chart. Figure 6.8 summarizes the Chart toolbar buttons.

Most buttons on the Chart toolbar apply a new format to the selected chart. For example, the Column chart tool (third from the left) reformats your line chart to the column chart illustrated in Figure 6.9.

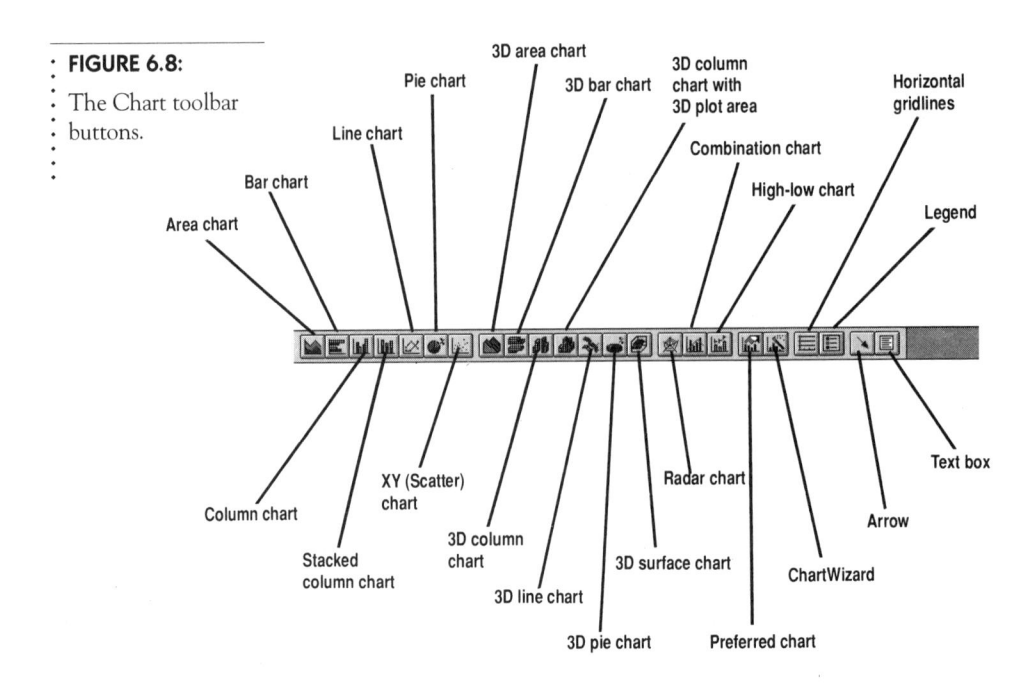

**FIGURE 6.8:** The Chart toolbar buttons.

Labels: Area chart, Bar chart, Line chart, Pie chart, 3D area chart, 3D bar chart, 3D column chart with 3D plot area, Combination chart, High-low chart, Horizontal gridlines, Legend, Column chart, Stacked column chart, XY (Scatter) chart, 3D column chart, 3D line chart, 3D pie chart, 3D surface chart, Radar chart, Preferred chart, ChartWizard, Arrow, Text box

*Understanding the Different Chart Types*

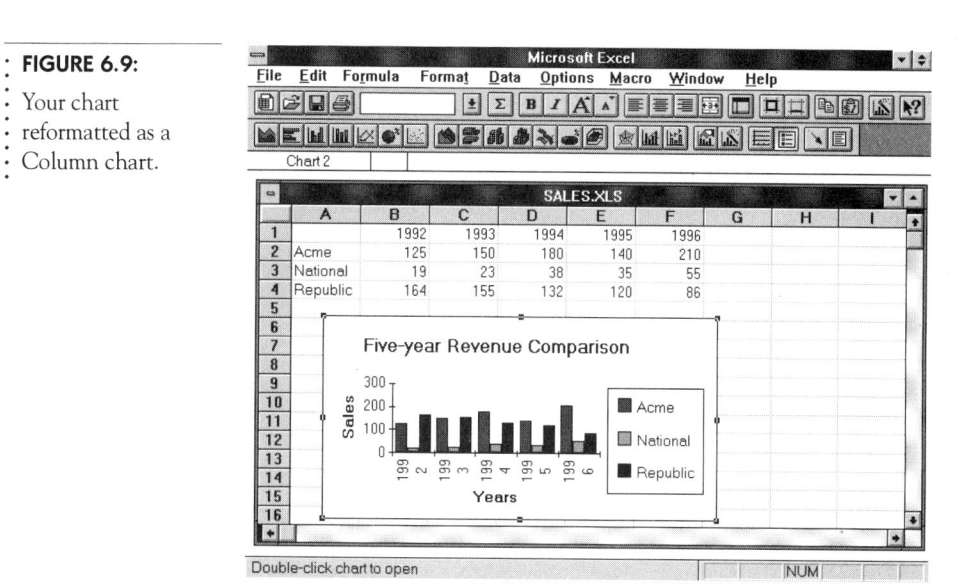

**FIGURE 6.9:**
Your chart reformatted as a Column chart.

When you select the ChartWizard tool, the ChartWizard dialog boxes are redisplayed so you can modify your answers to the ChartWizard's questions. The Gridlines tool adds these features when the format of your chart accepts them. The Legend tool places a legend on your chart. To add arrows, which you can move around with your mouse, use the Arrow tool. Free Text lets you freely enter any new text into your chart.

## UNDERSTANDING THE DIFFERENT CHART TYPES

In the second ChartWizard dialog (see Figure 6.3), you choose which of the thirteen chart types provided by Excel to use: Area charts, Bar charts, Column charts, Line charts, Pie charts, Radar, XY (Scatter), Combination, 3-D area, 3-D Bar, 3-D Column, 3-D Line, 3-D Pie, and 3-D Surface. The following guidelines will help you choose the appropriate chart type.

**69**

*Presenting Your Data with Charts*
**LESSON 6**

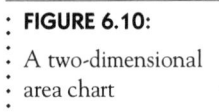

## USING TWO-DIMENSIONAL AND THREE-DIMENSIONAL AREA CHARTS

Area charts plot cumulative data series as lines. Figure 6.10 shows the five-year revenue data in an area chart. Excel first plots the data series for Acme. It then plots the data series line for National as the *sum* of the first and second data series. Excel plots the third data series' values as the sum of the first, second, and third data series. Finally, it fills in the areas between lines.

Because area charts plot data series cumulatively, they are most useful for showing the trend in the total data series. For example, in Figure 6.9, the only information clearly communicated is the total revenue of the three companies, Acme, National, and Republic.

Excel also provides a three-dimensional area chart, in several formats. Most formats simply use the third dimension of depth to make the plotted area look solid. The most effective three-dimensional area charts, however, use depth to organize the plotted areas, arranging the different data series' areas in order of increasing visual depth.

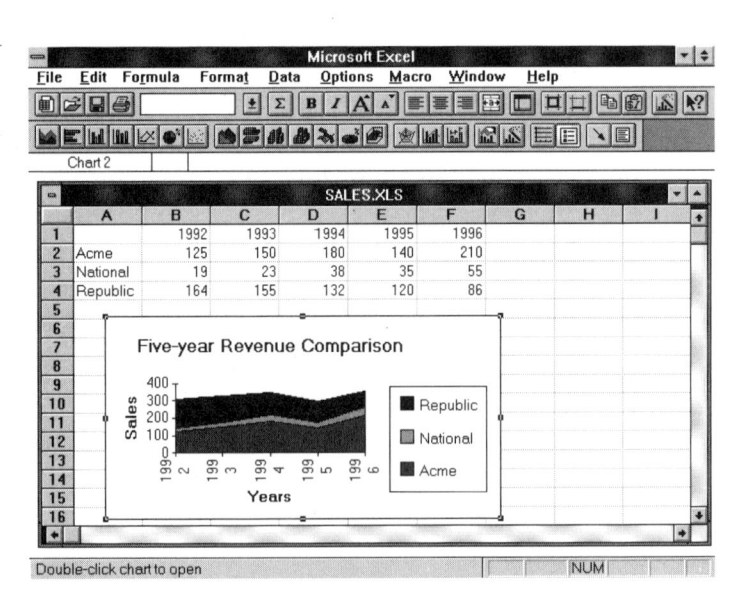

**FIGURE 6.10:**

A two-dimensional area chart

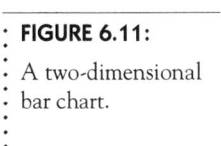

# USING TWO-DIMENSIONAL AND THREE-DIMENSIONAL BAR CHARTS

Bar charts plot each data series' points as horizontal bars, as shown in Figure 6.11. Because they don't use a horizontal category axis, bar charts are most useful for comparing two or more data series without the element of time, such as comparing revenues for the three companies for a single year. (Most people are used to seeing the horizontal axis used to show the passage of time.) In Figure 6.11, the vertical axis is used to show the passage of time—which is a little confusing.

Excel lets you graph data as both two-dimensional and three-dimensional bar charts. The only difference between a two-dimensional and a three-dimensional bar chart is that in a three-dimensional bar chart, Excel makes the bars look solid by adding the illusion of depth. In general, because a three-dimensional bar chart uses the third dimension only as a visual gimmick, it probably won't present your data more effectively or accurately.

**FIGURE 6.11:**
A two-dimensional bar chart.

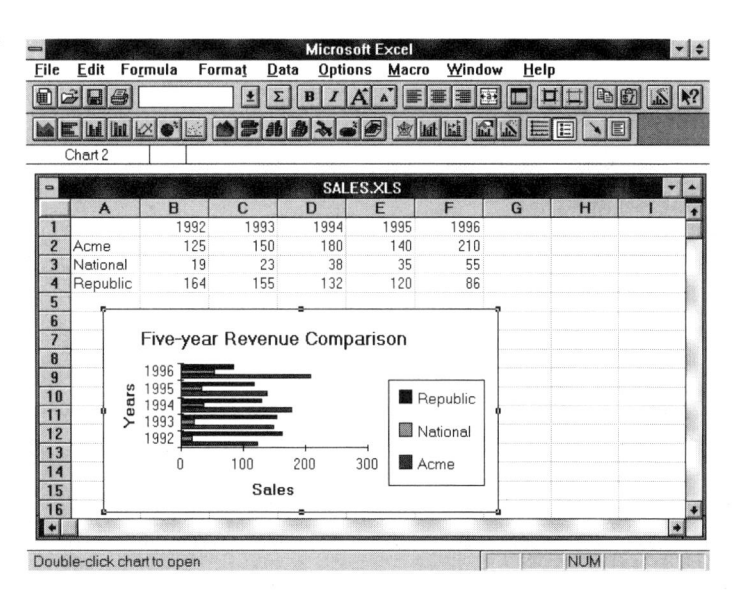

*Presenting Your Data with Charts*
**LESSON 6**

## USING TWO-DIMENSIONAL AND THREE-DIMENSIONAL COLUMN CHARTS

Column charts plot each data series values as vertical bars, as shown in Figure 6.9. Column charts, because they use a horizontal category axis, are most useful for time-series plots where you want to compare data points. You can use the category axis to show time. You can easily compare and calibrate the individual bars.

Excel also provides three-dimensional column charts. Many of these formats use the third dimension to make the plotted columns look solid—which only complicates the graphic without providing additional information. Some of the three-dimensional column charts, however, use depth to organize the plotted columns, arranging the different data series' columns in order of increasing visual depth.

## USING TWO-DIMENSIONAL AND THREE-DIMENSIONAL LINE CHARTS

Line charts, as you saw in Figure 6.7, plot each data series in a separate line. Because line charts use lines and a horizontal category axis, they are useful for showing trends over time. They tend, however, to de-emphasize the actual data point values. Excel also provides a three-dimensional line chart type. It plots ribbon-like lines using the third dimension to organize the plotted data series. This type of line chart is difficult to use well because the ribbon-like lines are difficult to compare to the chart axes.

## USING PIE CHARTS

Pie charts plot a single data series, with each data point represented as a slice of the pie. The size of the slice is determined by the ratio of the data point value to the total of all the data point values. A data point that's one-quarter of the total appears as a pie slice equal to one-quarter of the pie. Pie charts emphasize the relative sizes of a data series' points. Figure 6.12 shows a two-dimensional pie chart comparing the relative sizes of the 1992 revenues of Acme, National, and Republic.

Excel also provides a three-dimensional pie chart, which should be used with caution (if at all). To create the illusion of depth, Excel (and every other computer-based graphics application) tips the pie so part of the pie appears in the foreground

*Understanding the Different Chart Types*

**FIGURE 6.12:**

A two-dimensional pie chart.

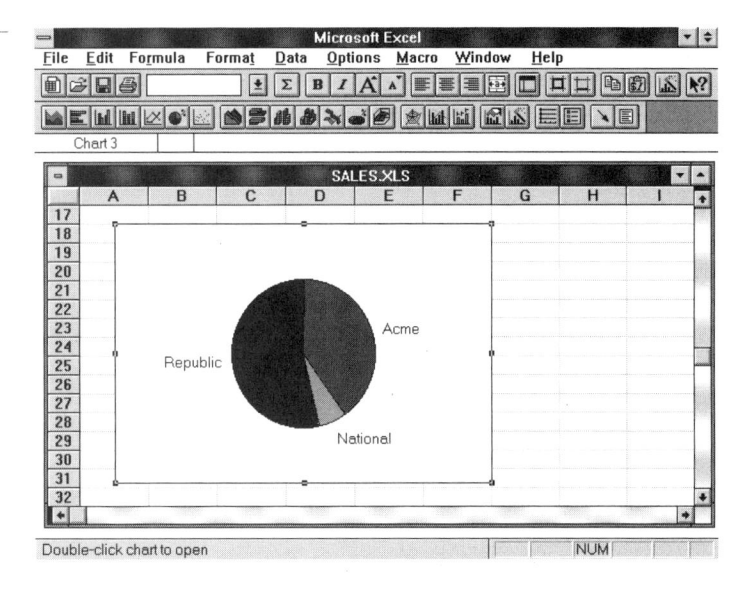

and part appears in the background. Unfortunately, pie slices in the foreground appear larger than they are and slices in the background appear smaller. Thus, it's impossible to compare the relative sizes of the different pie slices—which is, after all, the purpose of a pie chart. Even labeling the slices with their values doesn't seem to overcome the effect of the visual distortion.

## USING RADAR CHARTS

Radar charts use a separate value axis for each category, which makes them resemble a spider web or a radar screen. Look back at the dialog box in Figure 6.3 to see an example of a radar chart. Typically, you use radar charts for non-time-series data when you want to make it extremely easy to compare each category's data points. For example, if you wanted to plot exhaust emission data for three diesel engines and your categories were carbon dioxide, carbon monoxide, and unexpended diesel fuel, you might find using three category axes—one for each type of emission—helpful.

*Presenting Your Data with Charts*
**LESSON 6**

## USING SURFACE CHARTS

Surface charts plot data points on a three-dimensional grid. While surface charts are visually impressive, they should be planned carefully. The surface chart type is most useful for creating data maps, which arrange data points by geographic coordinates. For example if you wanted to create a data map that plotted population density by city blocks, you could use a surface chart. Your data series in this case might be north-south avenues and your categories might be west-east streets.

## USING XY, OR SCATTER, CHARTS

XY, or scatter, charts represent a particularly powerful data graphics tool, in that they let you visually show the correlation between pairs of data points. For example, using an XY chart, you can visually show the relationship between income and years of education. Typically, if you're going to use an XY chart to depict correlation, you will have previously validated the correlation using Excel's advanced regression tools.

## USING COMBINATION CHARTS

Combination charts combine two or more other chart types, such as a line chart and a column chart or a column chart and an area chart. You might use a combination chart if your different data series are best represented by different chart types—for example, you want to plot the trend in one data series with a line chart and the absolute values of another data series with a column chart.

Combination charts give you the option of using two value axes. This means you can more easily plot data series with greatly differing data point values—for example, you can plot interest rates as percentages and investment income in dollars.

# SAVING, RETRIEVING, AND PRINTING YOUR CHARTS

You can save, retrieve, and print your charts as independent files, but the easiest way to save, retrieve, and print a chart is by letting it remain a part of your worksheet.

## SAVING CHARTS AS INDEPENDENT FILES

To save your chart as an independent file, place your mouse pointer on it and double-click the left mouse button. Excel displays your chart in its own window, as shown in Figure 6.13. Use the File ➤ Save As to name and save your chart. Excel uses the file extension .XLC for charts.

To retrieve a chart saved as a separate file, simply use the Open command.

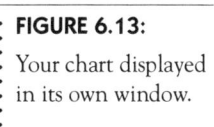

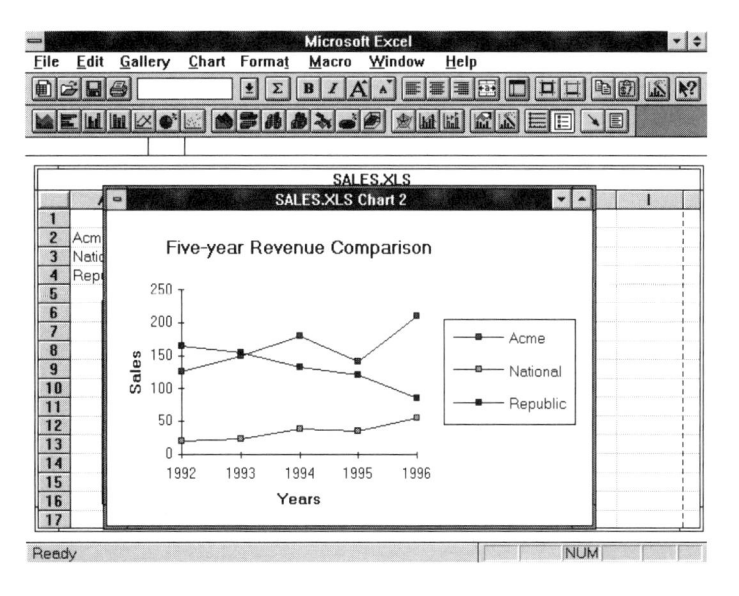

**FIGURE 6.13:**
Your chart displayed in its own window.

*Presenting Your Data with Charts*
**LESSON 6**

> **NOTE**
> 
> *When you work with a chart in its own window, Excel displays a slightly different version of the menu bar including commands specifically related to charts. For more information on the special chart menu bar and its commands, refer to the Excel on-line Help system.*

## PRINTING CHARTS AS SEPARATE ITEMS

You can print your charts as part of the worksheets they're placed on, or you can print them as separate items.

> **WARNING**
> 
> *When you want to print a chart as part of a worksheet, be sure the specific print area or range, if you've selected one, includes your chart.*

To print your chart as a separate item, place your mouse pointer on the chart and double-click the left mouse button. Excel displays your chart in its own window. With the chart window active, choose the File menu's Print command to initiate the printing process.

## LOOKING AHEAD

This lesson has given you a brief and practical overview of Excel's excellent charting features. For more information on the topics introduced in this lesson, refer to the following Reference entries:

- Charting
- Objects
- Toolbar

Lesson 7 shows you some basic macro techniques for automating repetitive worksheet tasks.

# 7

# Automating Your Work with Macros

**INTRODUCING**

*Creating a simple keystroke macros*

*Using the Record and Run commands*

*Creating a command macro*

A *macro* is a recorded series of keystrokes or commands. By running a macro, you can execute those keystrokes or commands automatically and accurately. Excel lets you create macros to automate simple, repetitive sequences of keystrokes, or to run applications as powerful as point-of-sale accounting and inventory management.

*Automating Your Work with Macros*
**LESSON 7**

# RECORDING AND RUNNING KEYSTROKE MACROS

This lesson shows you how to create and run a simple keystroke macro and a more complicated command macro. If you haven't already done so, start Excel and display a blank worksheet.

## THE RECORD COMMAND

The easiest way to create a macro is by using the Record command to record the actions you want to automate. Excel's Record command creates macros by recording keystrokes and other actions. To demonstrate the procedure, we can create a macro to enter the label International Amalgamated, Incorporated. Any text that you would otherwise need to type verbatim in many different places is a good candidate for recording as a macro. To create this label using the Macro Recorder, you would follow these steps:

1. Move the cell selector to the empty cell where you want the label entered.

2. Choose the Record command from the Macro menu to display the dialog box shown in Figure 7.1.

3. In the Name text box, enter a name for your macro, such as **Namer**. You can use any combination of letters and numbers to name your macro, but you can't use spaces.

4. To make running the macro even easier, you can enter a shortcut key that works with the Ctrl key to start your macro. Excel assigns letters in alphabetical order as default shortcut keys.

**FIGURE 7.1:**
The Record Macro dialog box.

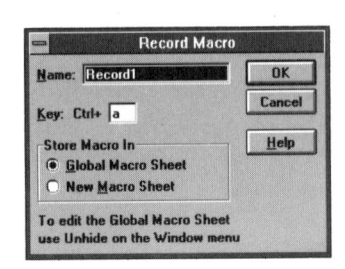

> **NOTE**
> 
> *Excel stores your macros in **macro sheets**, which resemble regular worksheet files but use the file extension .XLM. When you record a macro, the Store Macro In option buttons let you choose to store your macro in the GLOBAL.XLM file or in a separate new macro sheet file you can save, rename and open just like you would a regular worksheet file. If you want your macro available at all times, mark the Global Macro Sheet button. Macros used only with a particular project might be grouped into their own sheet, however.*

**5.** When the Record Macro dialog box is complete, select OK to start the recorder. To indicate you've turned on the recorder, Excel displays the word "Recording" on the status bar.

**6.** Type **International Amalgamated, Incorporated** and then press ↵. Figure 7.2 shows your worksheet with the label entered in cell A1.

**7.** Select the Stop Recorder command from the Macro menu to complete the process. You've just written your first macro.

**FIGURE 7.2:**
Your worksheet with the macro keystrokes entered.

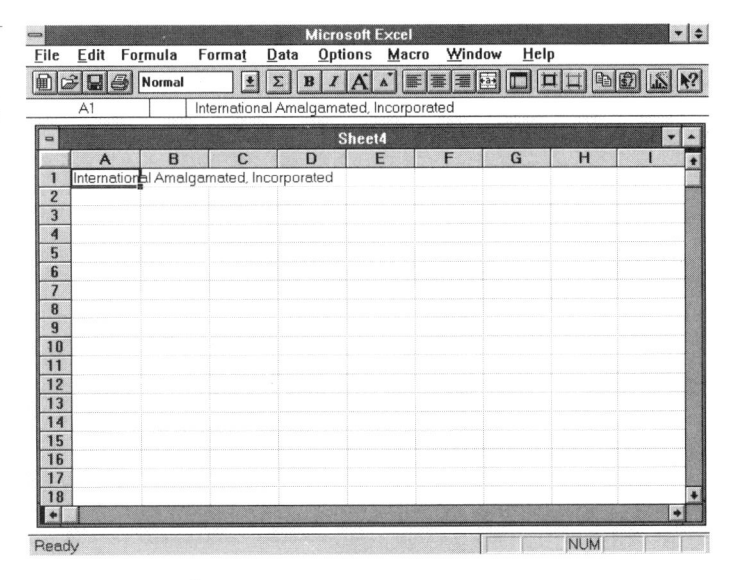

Automating Your Work with Macros
**LESSON 7**

> *The Macro Recorder doesn't record all commands and actions. It doesn't accept commands from the application window's control menu. Nor does it record commands you choose from the Macro menu. It also doesn't record your choices when you select the Cancel button on a dialog box. So, in the preceding keystroke macro, the only actions that Excel records are the keystrokes—and not the choosing of the macro menu commands Start Recorder and Stop Recorder.*

## THE RUN COMMAND

To run your macro, move the cell selector to an empty cell such as C3, and press the shortcut key combination you assigned (Ctrl-a is the default). Excel automatically enters the label you recorded, as shown in Figure 7.3.

You can also run your macro by selecting the Run command from the Macro menu. Excel displays the dialog box shown in Figure 7.4.

The Run list box shows the shortcut key, file name followed by an exclamation point, and the names of each of your macros. Figure 7.4 shows the letter "n" as the shortcut key and the word "namer" as the macro name. The Reference box shows the macro selected in the Run list box. Use the OK command button to run the selected macro.

**FIGURE 7.3:**

The worksheet after running your macro in cell C3.

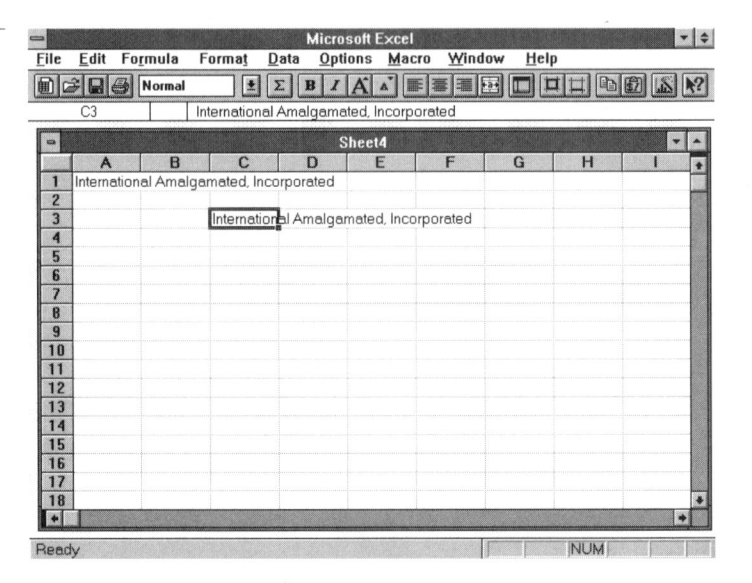

80

**FIGURE 7.4:**

The Run Macro dialog box.

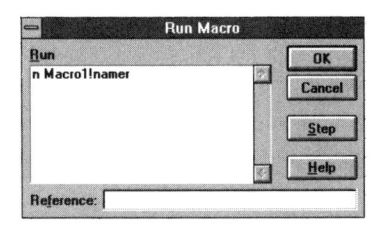

> *To verify the operation of your macros, use the Step command button to display the Single Step dialog box. This feature lets you step through a selected macro action-by-action, which makes it very useful when a complex macro is not doing what you expect. As you step through the macro, you can see where the trouble is.*

# MACRO RECORDER TIPS

The Record command also lets you record macros composed of other actions such as menu command choices, cell selector and cursor movements, and the selection of worksheet ranges. Before you use the Macro Recorder in these ways, however, you need to know a little more about how the recorder works.

***Recording Relative Cell References*** By default, Excel assumes that recorded cell selector movements should be absolute. When you record selector movement from one cell to another, Excel treats the action as if you used the Formula menu's Goto command. To record relative cell selector movements, or the specific methods and steps you used to get from one cell to another, choose the Relative Record command from the Macro menu. To return to the default setting, choose the Absolute Record command.

To understand the difference between these two ways of recording movement between cells, suppose you recording the action of moving the cell selector from cell A1 to cell A2. If you're recording the cell selector movements in absolute terms, Excel records the action as moving the cell selector to cell A2. If you're record movements in relative terms, Excel records the action as moving the cell selector down one row.

*Automating Your Work with Macros*
**LESSON 7**

***Pausing the Recorder*** To suspend your recording session temporarily, choose the Macro menu's Stop Recorder command. To start recording again, choose the Start Recorder command.

***Working with Macro Sheets*** As noted earlier, Excel stores macros in macro sheets, which resemble regular worksheet files. Macro sheets use the same techniques for printing, saving, and retrieving as regular worksheets. To retrieve a macro sheet file, use the Open command on the File menu. Remember, macro sheet files use an .XLM extension.

> *If you want to display a blank macro sheet so you can write a macro from scratch, choose the File menu's New command and select the Macro Sheet option from the dialog box. For more information on creating your own macro sheets from scratch, see* **Mastering Excel 4 for Windows**, *by Carl Townsend (SYBEX, 1992).*

To print a macro sheet, make its window active by selecting the document from the Window menu, and then choose the File menu's Print command. If you want to print a selected area of your macro sheet, use the Set Print Area command on the Options menu.

> *Excel hides the GLOBAL.XLM macro sheet document. To unhide it so you can make it active and print the macros you've stored in it, use the Window menu's Unhide command.*

To save a macro sheet, first make its window active, and then use the Save or Save As command on the File menu. Use the Save As command the first time you save your macro sheet so you can name it and specify its disk and directory location. Use the Save command for subsequent saves. Excel adds the .XLM file extension automatically.

> *For more information on saving, retrieving, and printing, see Lessons 1, 3, and 5.*

# WRITING A COMMAND MACRO

Keystroke macros, like the Namer macro, can be very useful if they let you automate keystroke sequences you repeatedly type. Keystrokes aren't the only things you can automate, however. You can also automate commands and command sequences. This means, of course, that you can also automate repetitive command sequences—a macro technique that puts you on the road to using macros as an application programming language.

To illustrate the procedure, we can write a command macro that enters the twelve month-end dates for a year into the adjacent cells in a row. If you're a business user of Excel, for example, you might end up doing this every time you created a budgeting worksheet or sales forecast. The advantage of automating this task should be obvious.

To write a command macro, you take the same basic steps as you do to write a keystroke macro. The only difference, in fact, is that rather than just typing keystrokes, you'll also be choosing commands.

> *The most expedient way to enter the month-end dates for the twelve months of the year is by using the Data Series command, so it's what you'll use for the macro. This command lets you enter a series of values into a worksheet range as long as they follow a predictable pattern. For more information on the Series command, refer to the Excel on-line Help system.*

To construct the command macro using the recorder, display an empty worksheet or the one you used with the keystroke macro. Next, choose the Macro menu's Relative Record command so that you record relative cell addresses and not absolute cell addresses. Then follow these steps:

**1.** Move the cell selector to cell B3.

*Automating Your Work with Macros*
**LESSON 7**

2. Choose the Record command from the Macro menu to display the dialog box shown in Figure 7.1.

3. Enter a name for your macro in the Name text box, such as Labeler.

4. As with keystroke macros, you can accept the default shortcut key or assign one of your own. When the Record Macro dialog box is complete, select OK to start the recorder. Excel displays the word "Recording" on the status bar.

5. Enter the formula =DATE(YEAR(NOW()),1,31). This formula, which uses several functions, calculates the date value for January 31 of the current year.

> *Excel lets you use values to represent dates and times: 1 for January 1, 1900, 2 for January 2, 1900, and so on all the way to 65,380 for December 31, 2078. This handy feature makes it easy to do date and time arithmetic. To make working with date and time values easier, Excel provides several handy tools: date and time formats so Excel can display date and time values that look like dates, automatic conversion of cell entries that look like dates into their equivalent values, and special date and time functions like the =DATE(), YEAR(), and NOW() functions used here. Refer to Chapter 2 for information on Excel's functions.*

6. Press ↵ to enter the formula into cell B3. Excel, because it knows the formula returns a date value, formats it to look like a date—such as 1/31/94.

7. Select the worksheet range B3:M3 and choose Data ➤ Series. Excel displays the Data Series dialog box, as shown in Figure 7.5.

8. To tell Excel that it should fill the selected range with end-of-month date values, mark the Date and Month radio buttons. Leave the other radio buttons set to their default values. (Your Data Series dialog box should look like the one shown in Figure 7.5 when you finish marking the radio buttons.)

9. Select OK on the Data Series dialog box. Excel fills the selected range with end-of-month date values for the current year.

10. Select the Stop Recorder command from the Macro menu to complete the process. You've just written your first command macro.

**FIGURE 7.5:**
The Data Series dialog box.

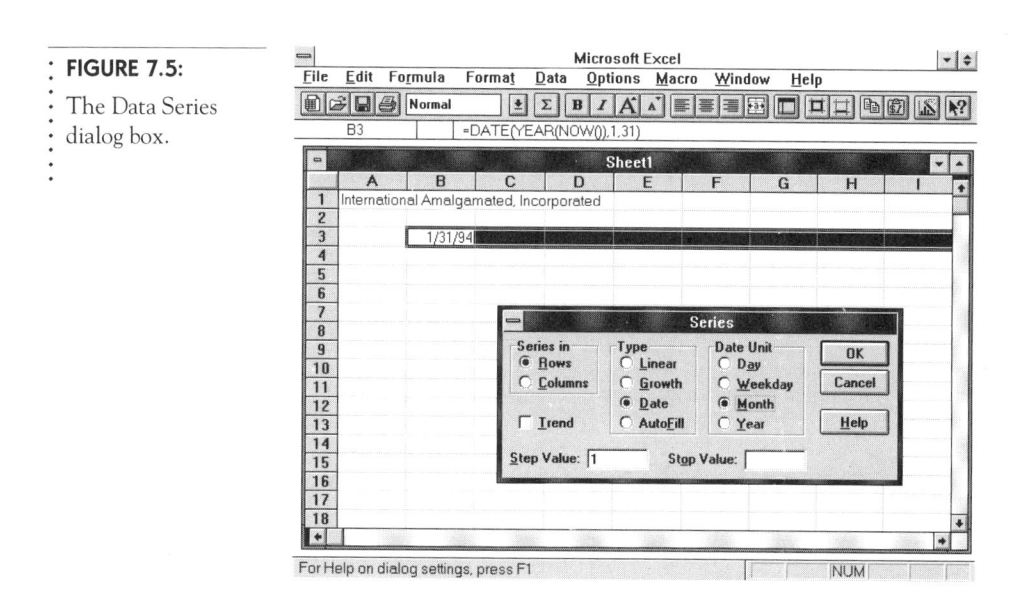

To use this macro again, all you need to do is position the cell selector in the cell where the January 31 date value should be entered. Then run the macro using either the Run command or its Ctrl-key equivalent.

Figure 7.6 shows the macro sheet Excel creates when you record the column-labeling macro. Cell A1 holds the macro name and the Ctrl-key shortcut. Cell A2

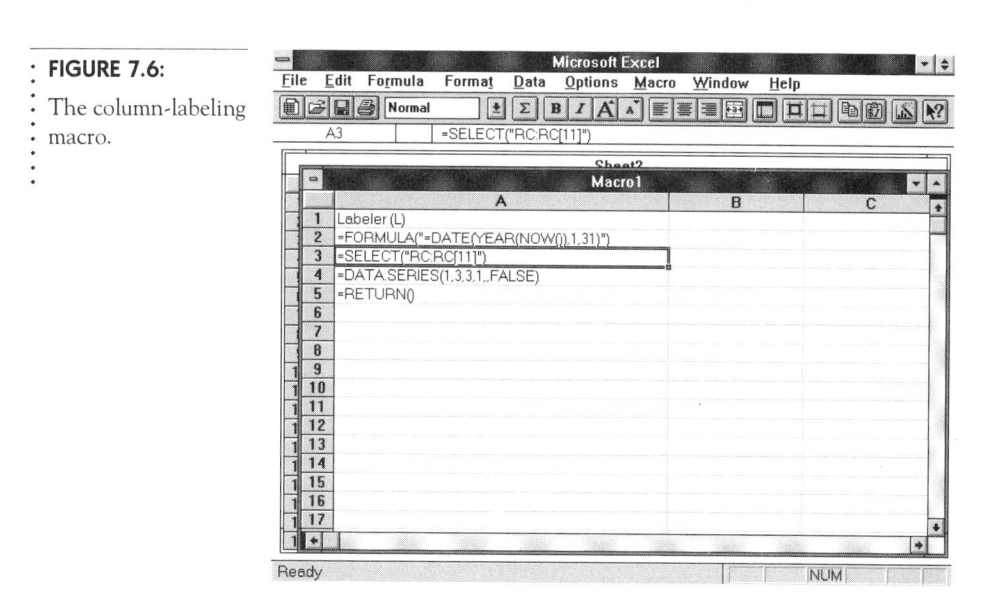

**FIGURE 7.6:**
The column-labeling macro.

*Automating Your Work with Macros*
**LESSON 7**

holds the command that tells Excel to enter the formula =DATE(YEAR (NOW()),1,31) into the active cell. Cell A3 tells Excel to select a worksheet range which includes the active cell and the eleven cells adjacent to it. Cell A4 runs the Data Series command. Finally, cell A5 tells Excel the macro is over, and that it should return control to you, the user.

Although this has been a fairly simple example, it should be clear that Excel's macro capability gives you the power to automate practically any series of commands and keystrokes. When you write command macros, you are, in effect, working with a programming language.

## LOOKING AHEAD

This lesson has introduced you to the quickest and most convenient way to create simple keystroke and command macros. For more information on the subjects covered in this lesson, consult the following Reference entries:

Add-ins

Grouping Worksheets and Macro Sheets

Macros

Series Values

Lesson 8 conveys some useful information on organizing your work with Excel's database capabilities.

# 8

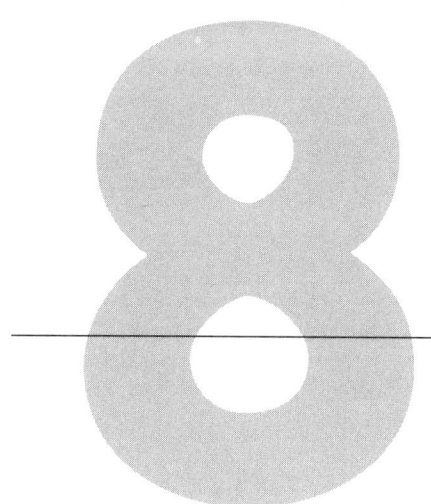

# ORGANIZING INFORMATION WITH DATABASES

**INTRODUCING**

*Creating databases in Excel*
*Editing and sorting your databases*
*Finding and extracting records*
*Printing, saving, and retrieving databases*

Databases are an excellent framework for organizing, storing, analyzing, and accessing information. While specialized database applications are capable of handling large volumes of complicated data, Excel's spreadsheet format and Data menu commands provide you with the basic tools for creating simple databases within the context of the program.

*Organizing Information with Databases*
**LESSON 8**

# CREATING DATABASES

Databases are collections of related information. Individual entries are called records, and each record contains one or more fields to hold data. This lesson shows how to create and work with a simple telephone directory database using Excel. If you haven't already done so, start Excel and display a blank worksheet.

## DEFINING YOUR DATABASE

To begin defining your database, take the following steps:

1. Enter the database field names in the first row of your worksheet. Each field name must be unique. For this example, you would use the names shown in Figure 8.1.

2. Select a range that includes the row with your field names and at least one empty row below. In Figure 8.1, the range should be A1:H2.

3. Choose Data ➤ Set Database. Your database is now defined and ready to receive data.

**FIGURE 8.1:**
Your worksheet with database field names entered.

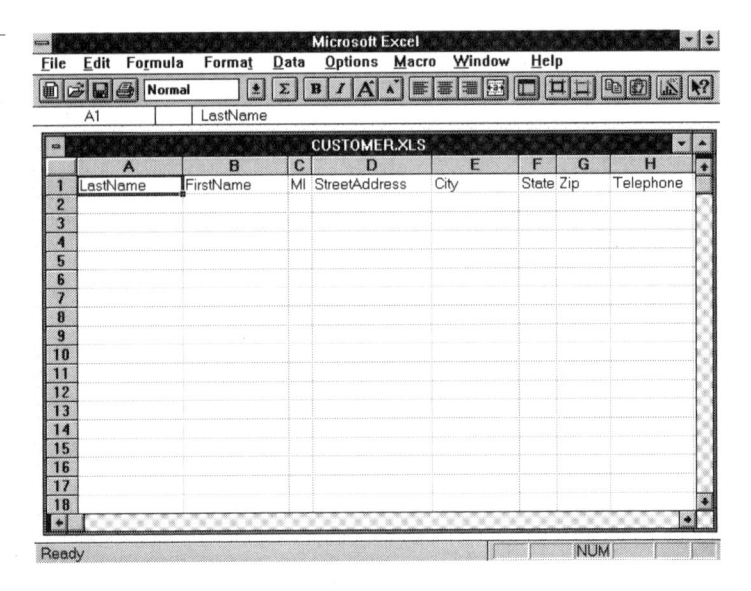

4. Normally, you will save your database, using File ➤ Save As. (For this example, saving is optional. You can use the worksheet name CUSTOMER.XLS.)

## ENTERING DATA

Choose Data ➤ Form to display the dialog box shown in Figure 8.2. Excel uses your database field names to label the text boxes.

To enter information into the fields of your database record, move the selection cursor to the appropriate text box and type in your data. To move between the text boxes, use the Tab and Shft-Tab keys or the mouse. When you've completed the record in each dialog box, press ↵. Excel enters the record into the next row of your worksheet range.

To add additional records, as shown in Figure 8.3, repeat this process. When all your records are entered, select the Close button.

> **TIP**
> *To clear all the entries in a dialog box so you can enter a corrected or new record, select the New command button.*

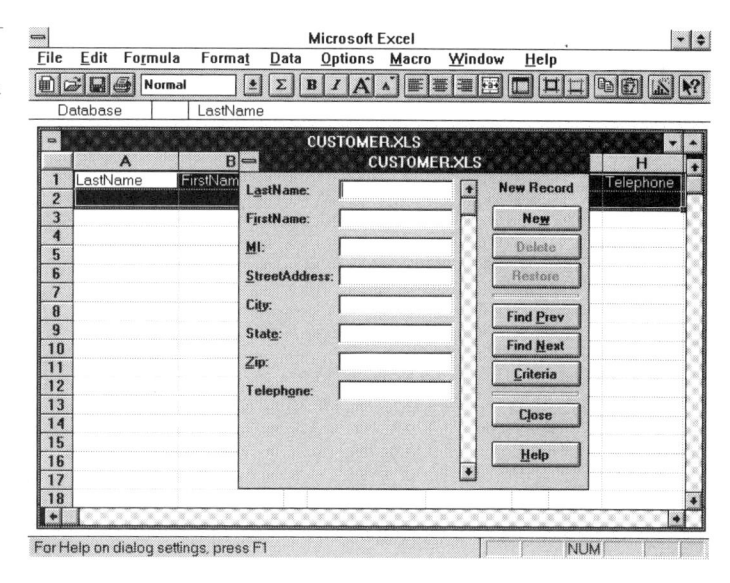

**FIGURE 8.2:**
Your customized data entry dialog box.

*Organizing Information with Databases*
**LESSON 8**

**FIGURE 8.3:**
Your completed CUSTOMER.XLS database.

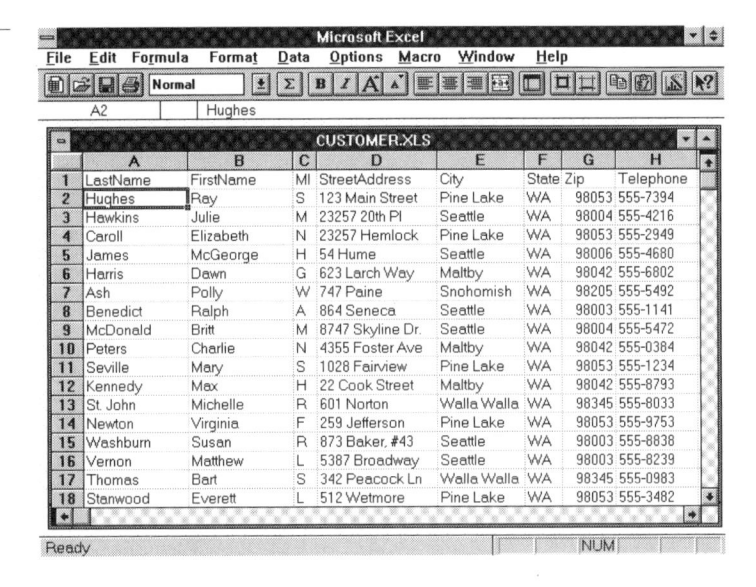

| | A | B | C | D | E | F | G | H |
|---|---|---|---|---|---|---|---|---|
| 1 | LastName | FirstName | MI | StreetAddress | City | State | Zip | Telephone |
| 2 | Hughes | Ray | S | 123 Main Street | Pine Lake | WA | 98053 | 555-7394 |
| 3 | Hawkins | Julie | M | 23257 20th Pl | Seattle | WA | 98004 | 555-4216 |
| 4 | Caroll | Elizabeth | N | 23257 Hemlock | Pine Lake | WA | 98053 | 555-2949 |
| 5 | James | McGeorge | H | 54 Hume | Seattle | WA | 98006 | 555-4680 |
| 6 | Harris | Dawn | G | 623 Larch Way | Maltby | WA | 98042 | 555-6802 |
| 7 | Ash | Polly | W | 747 Paine | Snohomish | WA | 98205 | 555-5492 |
| 8 | Benedict | Ralph | A | 864 Seneca | Seattle | WA | 98003 | 555-1141 |
| 9 | McDonald | Britt | M | 8747 Skyline Dr. | Seattle | WA | 98004 | 555-5472 |
| 10 | Peters | Charlie | N | 4355 Foster Ave | Maltby | WA | 98042 | 555-0384 |
| 11 | Seville | Mary | S | 1028 Fairview | Pine Lake | WA | 98053 | 555-1234 |
| 12 | Kennedy | Max | H | 22 Cook Street | Maltby | WA | 98042 | 555-8793 |
| 13 | St. John | Michelle | R | 601 Norton | Walla Walla | WA | 98345 | 555-8033 |
| 14 | Newton | Virginia | F | 259 Jefferson | Pine Lake | WA | 98053 | 555-9753 |
| 15 | Washburn | Susan | R | 873 Baker, #43 | Seattle | WA | 98003 | 555-8838 |
| 16 | Vernon | Matthew | L | 5387 Broadway | Seattle | WA | 98003 | 555-8239 |
| 17 | Thomas | Bart | S | 342 Peacock Ln | Walla Walla | WA | 98345 | 555-0983 |
| 18 | Stanwood | Everett | L | 512 Wetmore | Pine Lake | WA | 98053 | 555-3482 |

# WORKING WITH DATABASES

Excel provides a set of handy tools that let you easily update, retrieve, and organize your databases.

> **NOTE** *Microsoft Excel 4 comes with a separate application, called Q+E, that lets you access and update dBASE files, SQL Server files, Oracle files, and even Microsoft Excel files if they have a defined database. For more information on this application, refer to* **Mastering Excel 4 for Windows***, by Carl Townsend (SYBEX, 1992)*

## EDITING DATABASE RECORDS

You can edit your database the same way you edit any other worksheet, or you can use the Form command (as you did to enter the records initially). When you choose Data ➤ Form, Excel displays a dialog box like the one shown in Figure 8.2.

Display your records in the text boxes by using the PageUp and PageDn keys, the Up and Down arrow keys, the mouse and the scroll bar, or the Find Prev and Find Next command buttons. When the record you want to edit is displayed, make your changes by entering the correct data, and then display another database record or select the Close button to complete the process.

To undo your edits, select the Restore command button before displaying another record or using the Close button. To delete a record permanently, first find and display it on the Form dialog box, and then select the Delete command button.

> **TIP** *You can also use the Data menu's Delete command to delete multiple records that match certain criteria. Before using the Delete command, you must define your search criteria. See the section on finding and extracting records in this lesson.*

## SORTING YOUR DATABASE

Excel lets you sort your databases in a variety of ways to make them easier to use. For example, you would probably organize the CUSTOMER.XLS database alphabetically by name to make it easy to look up telephone numbers or addresses. To sort the CUSTOMER.XLS database by last name, you would take the following steps:

**1.** Select the worksheet range holding the database records you wish to sort, A2:H18. Note that you do not select the database field names.

> **TIP** *To select database records with your mouse, point to the first field of the first record and, holding down the left mouse button, drag the mouse pointer to the last field in the last record.*

**2.** Choose Data ➤ Sort. Excel displays the dialog box shown in Figure 8.4.

**3.** Mark the Rows option button to indicate that you've entered your records in rows.

**4.** Specify the first key you want used in sorting your records as the customer's last name by entering the cell address, $A$2, in the 1st Key box. Note that you must specify the key as an absolute reference.

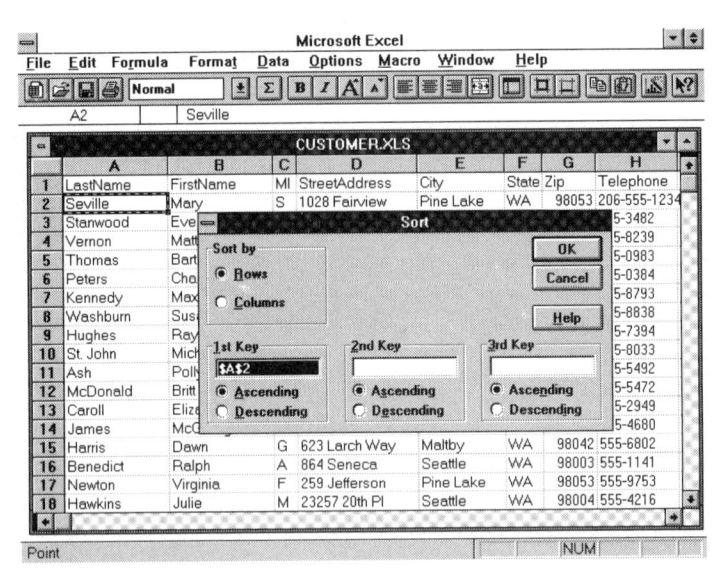

*Organizing Information with Databases*
**LESSON 8**

**FIGURE 8.4:**
The Sort dialog box.

**5.** Choose the Ascending option button to sort database records in A to Z order. Alternatively, you could choose the Descending option button to sort the database records in Z to A order.

> **TIP**
> *Use the 2nd and 3rd key settings to control sorting of records with identical 1st or 2nd keys. In our directory example, you could specify the first name field as a 2nd key to accommodate entries with the same last name.*

**6.** When your dialog box is complete, select OK to begin the sorting process. Figure 8.5 shows the CUSTOMER.XLS database sorted by last name.

> **TIP**
> *If you make a mistake sorting your database, use the Edit menu's Undo command to reverse the operation. Remember, the Undo command affects only the last action you performed.*

92

*Working with Databases*

**FIGURE 8.5:**
The sorted CUSTOMER.XLS database.

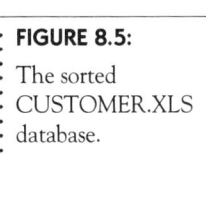

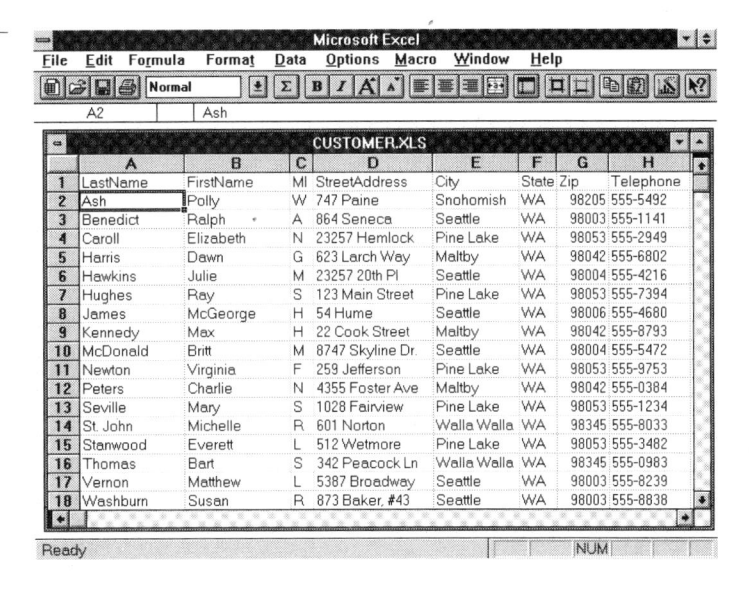

| | A | B | C | D | E | F | G | H |
|---|---|---|---|---|---|---|---|---|
| 1 | LastName | FirstName | MI | StreetAddress | City | State | Zip | Telephone |
| 2 | Ash | Polly | W | 747 Paine | Snohomish | WA | 98205 | 555-5492 |
| 3 | Benedict | Ralph | A | 864 Seneca | Seattle | WA | 98003 | 555-1141 |
| 4 | Caroll | Elizabeth | N | 23257 Hemlock | Pine Lake | WA | 98053 | 555-2949 |
| 5 | Harris | Dawn | G | 623 Larch Way | Maltby | WA | 98042 | 555-6802 |
| 6 | Hawkins | Julie | M | 23257 20th Pl | Seattle | WA | 98004 | 555-4216 |
| 7 | Hughes | Ray | S | 123 Main Street | Pine Lake | WA | 98053 | 555-7394 |
| 8 | James | McGeorge | H | 54 Hume | Seattle | WA | 98006 | 555-4680 |
| 9 | Kennedy | Max | H | 22 Cook Street | Maltby | WA | 98042 | 555-8793 |
| 10 | McDonald | Britt | M | 8747 Skyline Dr. | Seattle | WA | 98004 | 555-5472 |
| 11 | Newton | Virginia | F | 259 Jefferson | Pine Lake | WA | 98053 | 555-9753 |
| 12 | Peters | Charlie | N | 4355 Foster Ave | Maltby | WA | 98042 | 555-0384 |
| 13 | Seville | Mary | S | 1028 Fairview | Pine Lake | WA | 98053 | 555-1234 |
| 14 | St. John | Michelle | R | 601 Norton | Walla Walla | WA | 98345 | 555-8033 |
| 15 | Stanwood | Everett | L | 512 Wetmore | Pine Lake | WA | 98053 | 555-3482 |
| 16 | Thomas | Bart | S | 342 Peacock Ln | Walla Walla | WA | 98345 | 555-0983 |
| 17 | Vernon | Matthew | L | 5387 Broadway | Seattle | WA | 98003 | 555-8239 |
| 18 | Washburn | Susan | R | 873 Baker, #43 | Seattle | WA | 98003 | 555-8838 |

# FINDING AND EXTRACTING RECORDS

With large databases, it can be difficult to locate a specific record or group of records with common characteristics. Excel provides a simple way to search or query your database using the Form command's dialog box, and a more sophisticated method using specified search criteria and the Data menu's Find command.

## Querying Your Database

To query your database, display the Form command's dialog box and select the Criteria command button. Excel displays the Criteria dialog box shown in Figure 8.6. The Criteria dialog box resembles the Form dialog box because you can use any database field for querying.

To find a database record with the last name Seville, for example, enter **Seville** in the Last Name text box, and then select the Find Next or Find Prev command buttons to search your database. If Excel finds a record that matches your criteria, it displays the record in the Form dialog box.

To return to the Standard Form dialog box to enter, edit or delete your database records, select the Form button on the Criteria dialog box.

*Organizing Information with Databases*
**LESSON 8**

**FIGURE 8.6:**
The Criteria dialog box.

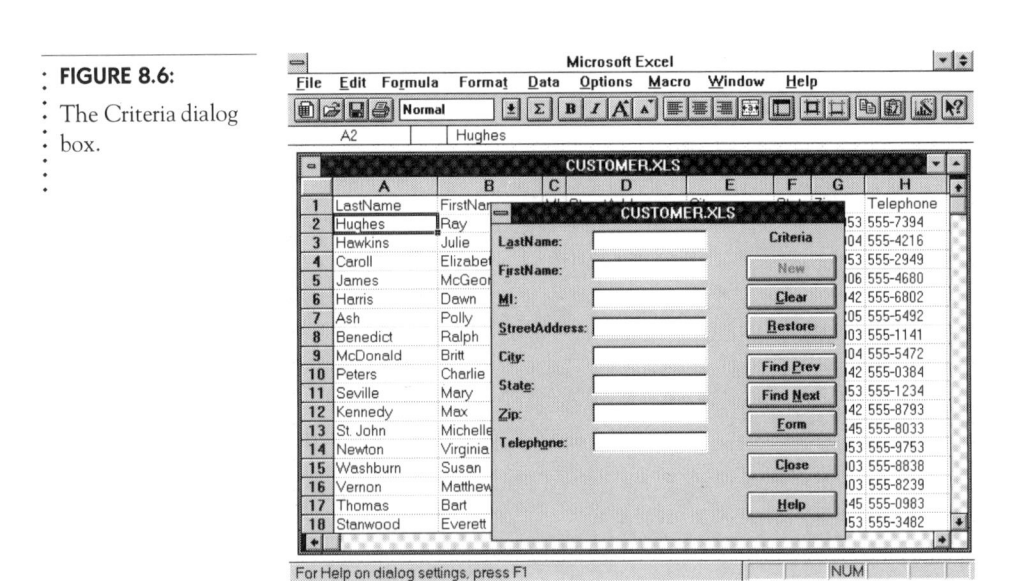

***Using Numeric Criteria*** To query your database for numeric values, the numeric criterion you enter must be preceded by a comparison operator. Excel accepts the following comparison operators:

|     |                          |
| --- | ------------------------ |
| =   | equal to                 |
| >   | greater than             |
| <   | less than                |
| <>  | not equal to             |
| >=  | greater than or equal to |
| <=  | less than or equal to    |

# THE FIND COMMAND

To locate a record using the Find command, follow these steps:

1. Enter your search criterion in a worksheet range, with the field name entered in one cell, and the criterion value entered in the cell directly below. If you were looking for the telephone number of someone named Stanwood, you would enter **Last Name**, which is the field name, in the first cell, and then the criterion value **Stanwood** in the cell directly below.

2. Identify the worksheet range holding your search criterion. Select the range, and then choose Data ➤ Set Criteria. Choose Data ➤ Find to begin the search operation. When Excel locates a record, it moves the cell selector to the first cell in the record. You can press ↵ to move between fields and find the specific entry you're seeking.

3. Choose Edit ➤ Repeat to continue the search operation, and use the Exit Find command on the Data menu to stop the process.

> *To specify multiple search criteria, simply enter additional values in the cells below the field name cell and use the cells in adjacent columns to enter additional field names. Select the entire range that defines your multiple search criteria, choose the Set Criteria command, and then the Find command to start the operation.*

## THE EXTRACT COMMAND

The Data menu's Extract command lets you extract records of a particular type and regroup them in another location on the same database worksheet. First, use the method you learned earlier to specify a search criterion for the records you want extracted. Next, tell Excel where to place your extracted records by copying and pasting the row with your database field names to a new location on your worksheet.

Select the range containing your copied and pasted field names, and then choose the Set Extract command from the Data menu. When you choose the Extract command from the Data menu, Excel copies all the records that match your extraction criterion to the rows below the selected field name row.

> *Excel may paste extracted records over existing data. If the cells containing your selection criteria are below your selected field name row, all the records in your database may be extracted if the criterion cells are pasted over. You can limit the scope of your operation by including a specific number of empty rows below the field name row in your selected range.*

*Organizing Information with Databases*
**LESSON 8**

# PRINTING, SAVING, AND RETRIEVING DATABASE FILES

Since databases are essentially worksheets, you can use the same techniques to print, save, and retrieve them. Databases even use the same .XLS file extension.

To print a database, use the File menu's Print command. You can also use the Option menu's Set Print Area command to designate a specific worksheet range for printing.

To save a database, use the File menu's Save As and Save commands. To retrieve a database, use the File menu's Open command. Locate and identify your database file on the File Open dialog box, and select OK to complete the process.

# LOOKING AHEAD

This lesson has given you a quick overview of creating and working with Excel databases. For more information on the topics introduced in this lesson, refer to the following Reference entries:

Databases

Q+E Application

Sorting Worksheet Data

If you've completed this and each of the preceding lessons in the Step-by-Step section of this book, you now possess the basic skills necessary to work with Excel on a practical level. However, you'll also find it helpful to understand how Excel, Windows, and other Windows applications work together. That is the topic of the next lesson.

# *E*XCEL AND WINDOWS

**INTRODUCING**

*Multitasking*

*Working with the Print Manager application*

*Sharing data with Object Linking and Embedding*

Windows supports your use of Excel in many important ways, such as multitasking, printing, and sharing of data. Knowing about these things isn't essential for using Excel, but it will make using Excel easier.

Excel and Windows
**LESSON 9**

# RUNNING MULTIPLE APPLICATIONS

The Windows operating environment lets you run more than one application at a time. For example, you can run Excel and also a word-processing application like Word for Windows or WordPerfect. To run more than one application—multitasking, in computer jargon—you use the Control menu's Switch To command.

To use the Switch To command from inside Excel, follow these steps:

1. Click the control box on the Excel application window to activate its Control menu. Figure 9.1 shows the Application window's Control menu displayed.

2. Choose the Switch To command. Windows displays the Task List dialog box, as shown in Figure 9.2.

3. Select the Program Manager item from the Task List either by double-clicking it or by highlighting it with the arrow keys and then clicking the Switch To command button. Windows displays your Program Manager window, similar to the one shown in Figure 9.3.

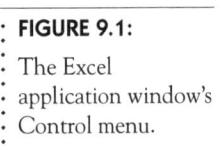

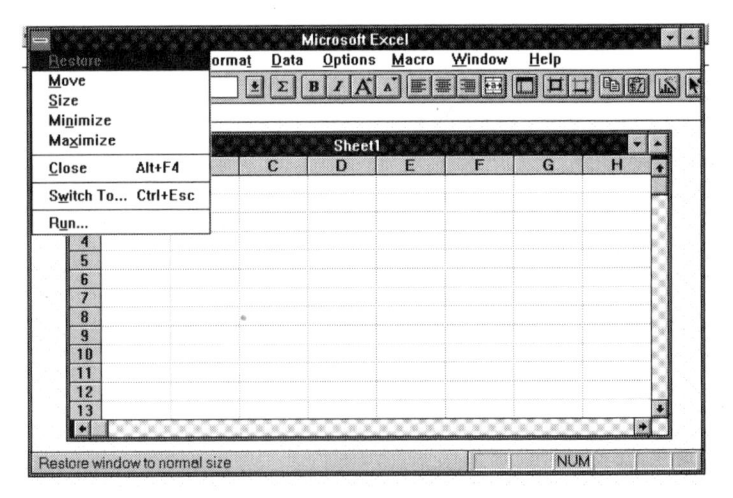

**FIGURE 9.1:**

The Excel application window's Control menu.

*Running Multiple Applications*

**FIGURE 9.2:**

The Task List dialog box.

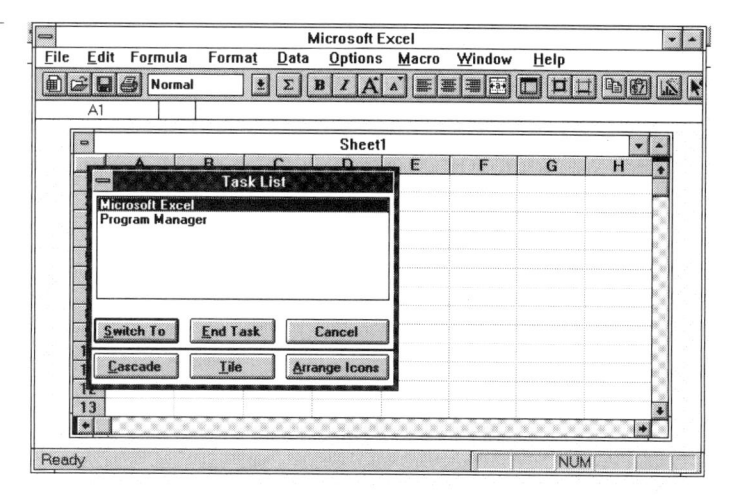

**FIGURE 9.3:**

The Program Manager window.

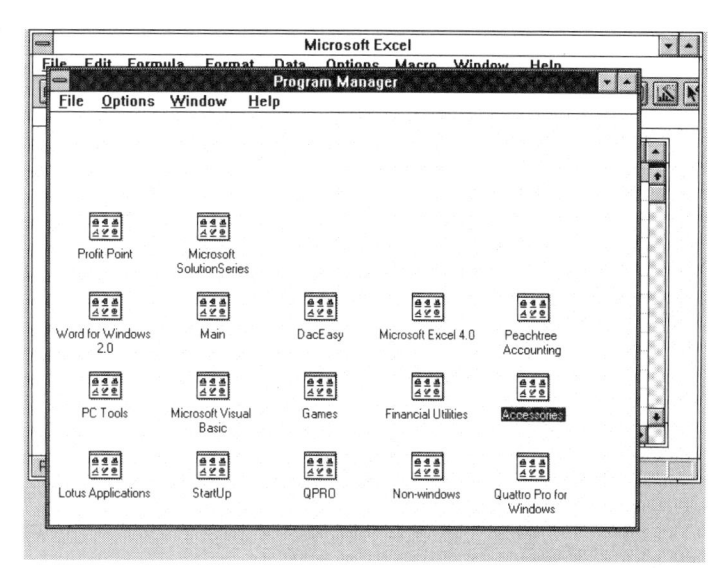

4. Use the Program Manager to start another application just as you start Excel. For example, to start the Windows Write application, display the Accessories program group and double-click the Write icon. Windows starts Write, which means it's now running two applications, Excel and Write.

*Excel and Windows*
**LESSON 9**

> *The Task List dialog box, shown in Figure 9.2, also helps you manage the applications you're running under Windows. Use the End Task command button as a last-resort method of exiting from applications that won't respond to your commands. Use the Cancel command button to close the Task List dialog box. Use the Cascade command button to arrange the running application's windows in a stack. Use the Tile command button to arrange the running application's windows in side-by-side windows. Use the Arrange Icons command button when you've minimized application windows and want to rearrange these icons into neat rows.*

Once you're running multiple Windows applications, you can display the Task List dialog box at any time by choosing the Switch To command from the active application's control menu. You can also use the short-cut combination for the Switch To command, Ctrl-Esc.

> *Only application window Control menus include the Switch To command. Document window control menus, like the ones used to display Excel worksheets, don't include it.*

# UNDERSTANDING THE PRINT MANAGER

Once you understand the Windows multitasking capability, it's easier to understand how Excel prints documents. When you choose the Print command from Excel's File menu, Excel doesn't actually print the document. Rather, it creates a copy, or spool file, of whatever it is you want to print, starts the Print Manager application, and then tells the Print Manager to print the spool file. If you're printing several documents, Print Manager prints them in the order the spool files were created. This whole sequence of events is transparent unless there's a problem.

## TROUBLESHOOTING WITH PRINT MANAGER

When there is problem—such as the printer not being turned on or an empty paper tray—the Print Manager pauses and displays a message box saying something like, "Printer Not Ready."

*Understanding the Print Manager*

When this occurs, first correct the problem by, for example, turning on the printer or adding paper. What happens next depends on the problem and the version of Windows you're running. If you're running Windows 3.1 or higher, sometimes all you have to do is correct the problem and select OK on the message box. Often, the Print Manager then resumes printing.

If the Print Manager doesn't resume printing after you correct the problem, however, you need to switch to the Print Manager application. Switch to Program Manager as described earlier in the lesson, and select the Print Manager icon from the Main group. You'll see the Print Manager application window, as shown in Figure 9.4.

Typically, printer problem-solving requires only that you use the three command buttons shown on the Print Manager's window: Pause, Resume, and Delete.

The Resume command button restarts a printer that stopped printing because of a problem. If you're connected to more than one printer, you'll need to select the appropriate one before choosing Resume. The Print Manager will restart and complete printing each of the spool files in its queue. (A printer's queue simply consists of the spool files it needs to print.)

The Delete command button lets you remove a spool file from a printer's queue. To use Delete, first click on the spool file you want to remove. Then choose Delete.

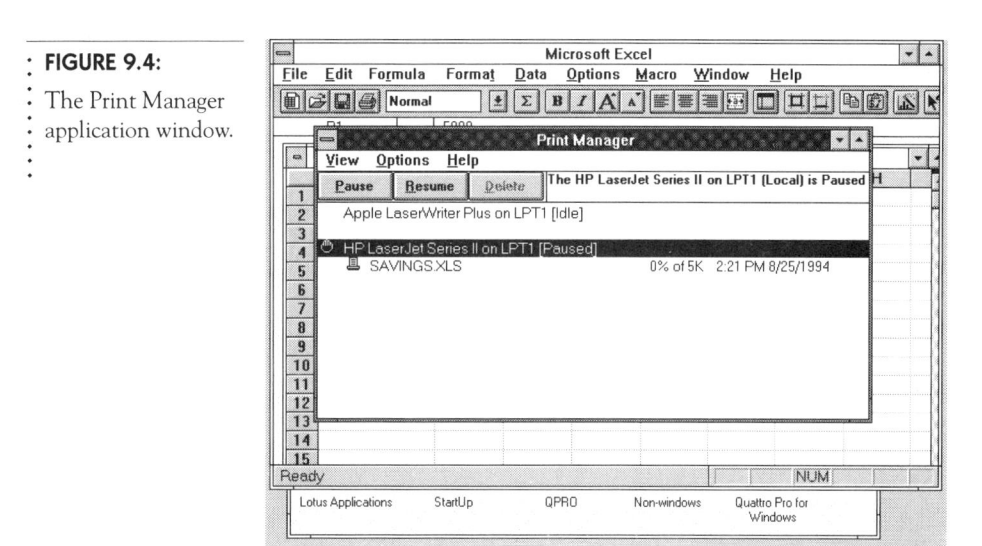

**FIGURE 9.4:**

The Print Manager application window.

**101**

Excel and Windows
**LESSON 9**

The Pause command button, of course, lets you suspend a printer's operation. To use Pause, select the printer you want to suspend, then choose Pause. To later restart the printer, use Resume.

# SHARING DATA USING OBJECT LINKING AND EMBEDDING

One of the major strengths of the Windows operating environment is that you can easily share data between applications. In Windows 3.1 and later, the way you do this is with object linking and embedding, or OLE (pronounced oh-lay!). Because OLE provides a very easy method for moving Excel charts and worksheets to other Windows applications—like your word processor—it's worth trying out an example. Here we will use the Write accessory, simply because everyone who has Windows has this word processor. If you've got another Windows word processor such as Word or WordPerfect, of course, you won't be using Write. Object linking and embedding works in the same basic way for almost all Windows applications, however. If you have questions about a particular application, refer to its documentation.

> *Even though Excel 4.0 and Windows 3.1 support Dynamic Data Exchange, or DDE, OLE makes DDE obsolete for most users. With OLE, Windows keeps track of source and destination applications and documents for you.*

To provide a concrete example of how OLE works, build the simple worksheet shown in Figure 9.5. Enter and format the values shown in the range B1:B3. Then, enter the formula =B1*(1+B2)^B3 into cell B5. As the figure labels indicate, the formula in cell B5 estimates the future value an investor accumulates by putting away $2,000 and then letting this investment accrue 8% interest for 25 years.

*Sharing Data using Object Linking and Embedding*

**FIGURE 9.5:**

A sample worksheet you can use to learn about OLE.

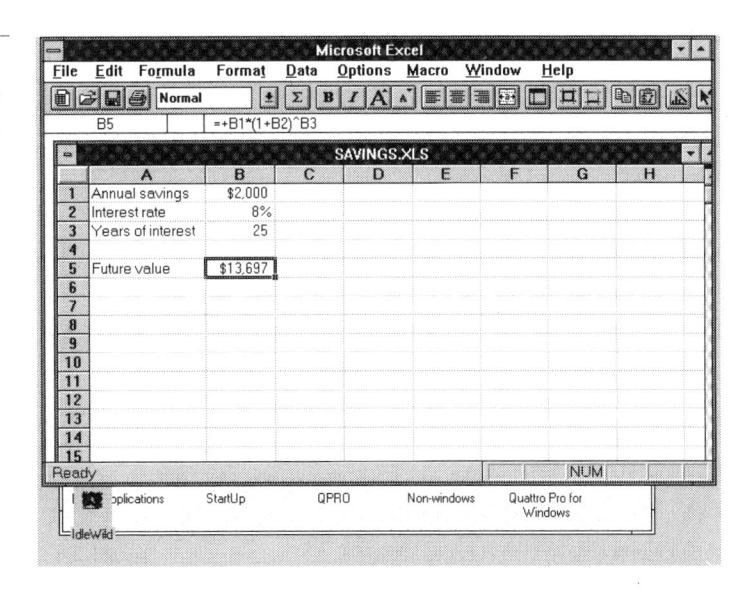

> To construct the worksheet in Figure 9.5, you need to know how to enter labels, values, and formulas. You also need to know how to format cells. Refer to Lessons 1, 2 and 4 if you have questions. To adjust the number of digits displayed for dollar amounts, choose Format ➤ Numbers.

Now suppose that after constructing the worksheet shown in Figure 9.5, you decide to include the worksheet as a table in a report you're writing using the Windows Write accessory. To do this using OLE, you would take the following steps:

**1.** Select the range A1:B5 in the Excel worksheet.

**2.** In Excel, choose Edit ➤ Copy. Excel makes a copy of the selected worksheet range and stores it on the Windows Clipboard.

**3.** Using the Switch To command, start the Windows Write accessory. (If you have questions about how to do this, refer to the earlier discussion of Running Multiple Applications.) Figure 9.6 shows the Write document window.

**103**

*Excel and Windows*
**LESSON 9**

**FIGURE 9.6:**
The empty Write document window.

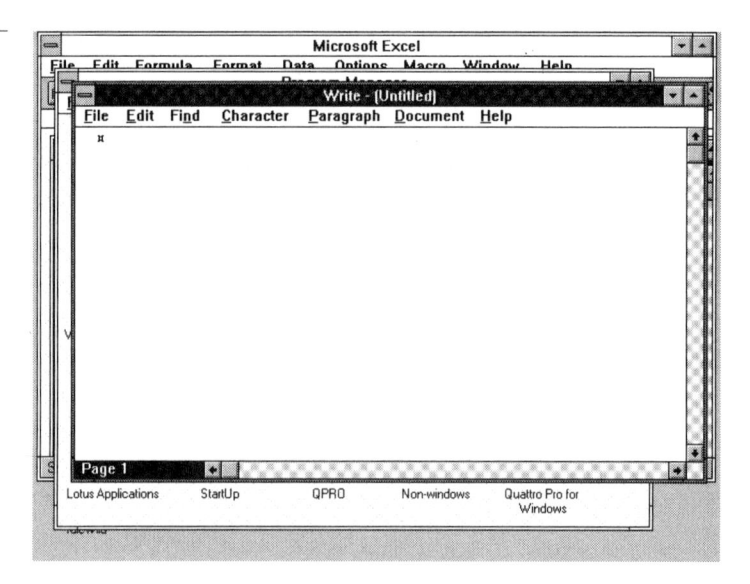

> Typically, of course, you would be probably paste a piece of an Excel worksheet into a word-processing document that wasn't empty. The investment future value table shown in Figure 9.5, for example, might go into a document that described an investment.

**4.** Choose Paste Special from the Write application's Edit menu. Write displays the dialog box shown in Figure 9.7.

**5.** From the Data Type list box select Bitmap, the format Write needs for linking and embedding. (Other Windows applications may accept Excel worksheets in other formats.)

**6.** To paste an embedded copy of the selected worksheet range, select the Paste command button. Or, to paste a linked copy of the selected worksheet range, select the Paste Link command button. (We'll discuss the difference in a moment.) Write pastes the copy of the selected worksheet range into the Write document. Figure 9.8 shows the pasted worksheet range.

Windows remembers the document that's the source of embedded and linked objects—SAVINGS.XLS in this illustration. Because of this connection, you can

*Sharing Data using Object Linking and Embedding*

**FIGURE 9.7:**

The Write application's Paste Special dialog box.

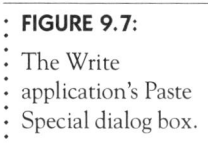

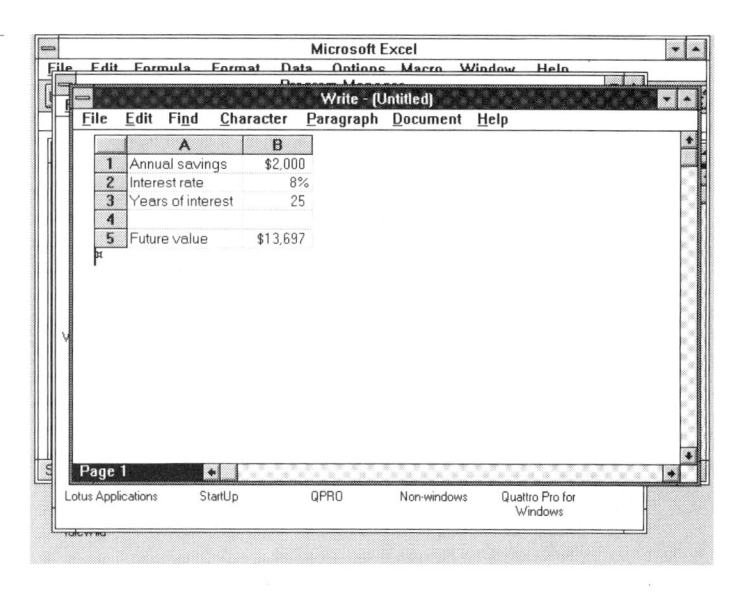

redisplay a source document simply by double-clicking on the object in its destination document. For example, if in the Write document you double-clicked on the future value worksheet shown in Figure 9.8, Windows would start Excel and then open the SAVINGS.XLS worksheet.

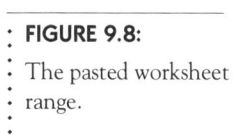

**FIGURE 9.8:**

The pasted worksheet range.

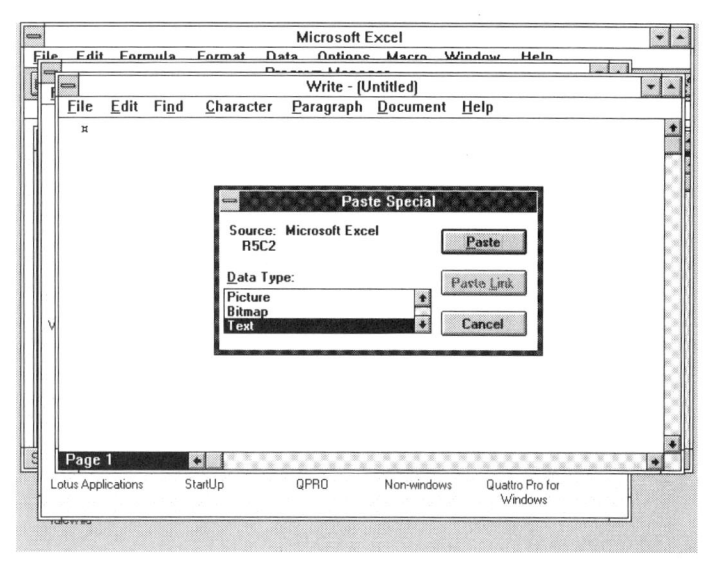

**105**

*Excel and Windows*
**LESSON 9**

## EMBEDDING VS. LINKING

You need to understand the difference between embedded objects and linked objects, but the difference isn't hard to grasp. An *embedded* copy won't change if the source document changes—such as if you recalculate using a different interest rate. A *linked* copy will change if the source document changes. For example, suppose you link the selected worksheet range pasted into the Write document and you change the interest rate in the Excel worksheet from 8% to 9%. Excel updates the formula in cell B5 to use the new value. Then, Windows updates the linked object in the Write document to reflect the changes you made to the source document.

## LOOKING AHEAD

This lesson has given you a quick overview of three important Windows topics: multitasking, using the Print Manager, and sharing data with object linking and embedding. For more information on these and other topics related to the Windows environment, see the following Reference entries:

    Application Windows
    Copying Data to the Clipboard
    Cutting Data to the Clipboard
    Object Linking and Embedding
    Pasting Data from the Clipboard
    Windows

If you've completed the lessons in the Step-by-Step section of this book, you should now possess both the Excel and the Windows skills necessary to employ Excel as a powerful business tool. As you work with Excel and broaden your understanding of its powerful features, feel free to consult the Reference section to answer any questions that may arise.

# PART II

# Alphabetical Reference

# Add-INS

**MENU PATH** Options ➤ Add-ins

The Add-ins command lets you specify which add-in macro files Excel should open whenever it starts. Opening the add-in macro files as part of starting Excel allows you to use the add-in macros any time you want.

By default, Excel opens several add-in macros, including macros to run the Solver command, the Scenario Manager command, and the Analysis Tools command. There are also more than a dozen other add-in macros that come with Excel.

**See Also** Analysis Tools, Modeling, Q + E Application

# Analysis TOOLS

**MENU PATH** Options ➤ Analysis Tools

The Options menu's Analysis Tools command displays a list of the special engineering, financial, and statistical tools provided in the Analysis Toolpack Add-in. To use one of these tools, choose the Analysis Tools command, select the tool you want from the list Excel displays, and then respond to Excel's prompts.

**NOTE** The Analysis Toolpack includes two engineering tools (Fourier Analysis and Sampling) and 17 other tools for making financial, and statistical calculations.

# Annotating CELLS

**MENU PATH** Formula ➤ Note

**SHORTCUT** Shift-F2

♦ APPLICATION WINDOWS

The Note command lets you attach textual notes to document or explain the contents of a cell. Cell notes can be edited and printed much like other Excel documents. Choose the Note command from the Formula menu to display the Cell Note dialog box.

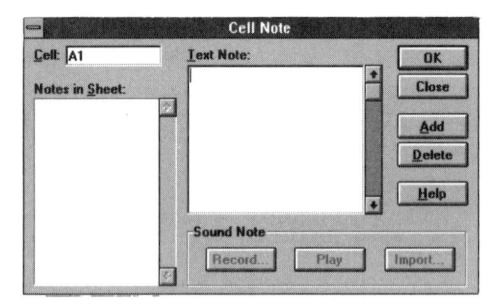

To attach a note to a cell, enter the cell address in the Cell text box and then type the note in the Text Note box.

**NOTE** If you select a cell before selecting the Note command, Excel automatically enters the cell's address in the Cell Note dialog box.

To see your cell notes, choose the Note command, and select the cell from the Notes in Sheet list to display the note in the Text Note box.

Cells that have attached notes are marked with a small red square on the upper-right corner when displayed on a worksheet.

For more information on how to use the Sound Note command buttons, consult your *Microsoft Excel User Guide*.

# APPLICATION WINDOWS

In the Windows operating environment, each application is displayed in its own window, called an application window. It is this window you see when you start an application like Excel. Applications use their application windows to display menu bars and any document windows.

110

You can use the Workspace Settings command to control the appearance of your Excel application window.

## TO CONTROL WORKSPACE SETTINGS

**MENU PATH**  Options ➤ Workspace

The Workspace command controls how the Excel application window appears during an Excel session. You can designate how rows and columns are identified; whether the status bar, scroll bars, and formula bars appear; how the Info window looks, and if cell notes are flagged.

The Workspace command also gives you the ability to change several of the mechanical aspects of Excel. You can tell Excel to automatically enter decimal points, change the way the menu bar is activated, and specify an alternate set of navigation keys.

**See Also**  Document Window, Windows

## AUTOMATIC BACKUP

When Excel saves a file for the second time, it replaces the existing file on disk with a new version of the file in memory. Excel provides you with the option of creating a backup copy of the previous version, however. To create backup copies, use the Options command button on the File Save As dialog box. The File Save Options dialog box, which Excel displays if you select the Options command button, includes a check box you can mark to direct Excel to create backup files. Excel names the backup using the same file name and the file extension .BAK.

**See Also**  Saving a File

◆ CELL CHARACTERISTICS

# CALCULATING WORKSHEETS

**MENU PATH** Options ➤ Calculation

**SHORTCUT** F9

The Options menu's Calculation command lets you control whether worksheet recalculation is automatically initiated by Excel or manually initiated by the user. You can also use the Calculation command to control more esoteric aspects of worksheet calculation, such as how many times circular references are iteratively recalculated and how linked formulas are recalculated.

**NOTE** To initiate recalculation manually, press F9 or select the Calc Now or Calc Doc buttons on the Calculation dialog box.

# CELL ADDRESS

Each cell in a worksheet has an address that consists of the column letter and the row number. The cell at the intersection of column B and row 2, for example, is named B2. You use cell addresses to refer to cells in response to command prompts and to use cell contents in formulas.

**See Also** Cell Reference, Formulas, Range Names

# CELL CHARACTERISTICS

**MENU PATH** Formula ➤ Select Special

The Select Special command selects cells with certain specified characteristics. To use the command, follow these steps:

1. Select the worksheet range you want to search.

**2.** Choose the Select Special Command from the Formula menu to display the Select Special dialog box.

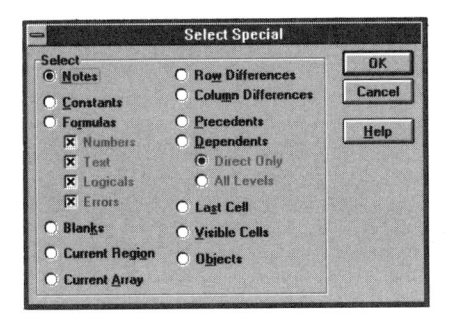

**3.** Mark the appropriate option buttons to locate:

- Cells with notes attached.
- Constants specified with the Numbers, Text, Logical Values, and Errors check boxes.
- Formulas that return results specified with the Numbers, Text, Logical Values, and Errors check boxes.
- Blanks or empty cells.
- The Current Region or the rectangle that surrounds the active cell.
- The Current Array that includes the active cell.
- The Row Differences of cells whose contents differ from those in the column to the left.
- The Column Differences of cells whose contents differ from those in the row above.
- The Precedents upon which formulas in the selected range depend, specified with the Direct Only or All Levels buttons.
- The Dependents of cells with formulas in the selected range, specified with the Direct Only or the All Levels buttons.
- The Last Cell at the intersection of the right-most column and bottom-most row to hold data or be formatted.
- The Visible Cells in the selected range.
- The Objects imbedded in the worksheet.

♦ CHARTING

    **4.** Select OK to complete the process.

    **See Also** Finding Cell Data, Replacing Cell Data

# CELL REFERENCE

A cell reference is simply a cell address or range name. You use cell references to construct formulas that use the contents of cells. Cell references can be either *relative* or *absolute*. Use relative cell references when you want Excel to adjust the reference's column letters and row numbers as the reference is copied. Use absolute cell references when you don't want Excel to adjust the reference's column letters and row numbers as the reference is copied. To make a column letter or row number absolute, precede it with the dollar sign.

    **See Also** Cell Address, Range Names

# CHARTING

    **SHORTCUT** ChartWizard tool

Excel lets you plot worksheet data using two-dimensional and three-dimensional data graphics, including area charts, bar charts, column charts, line charts, and pie charts. The easiest way to create charts in Excel is by using the ChartWizard.

## TO USE CHARTWIZARD

Using the Excel ChartWizard, you can easily and quickly create charts that plot worksheet data. To use the ChartWizard, follow these steps:

    **1.** Enter the data you want to plot in an Excel worksheet.

    **2.** Select the worksheet range that holds the data you want to chart. Include any row or column headings in your selection.

3. Select the ChartWizard tool from the toolbar. Excel changes your mouse pointer to a cross-hair.

4. Point the cross-hair to the upper-left corner of the range where you want your chart placed. Then, holding down the left mouse button, drag the cross-hair to the lower-right corner. Excel draws a box to show the placement of your chart and displays the first of five ChartWizard dialog boxes.

5. Select the Next button. Excel displays the second ChartWizard dialog box, which shows the thirteen basic chart types available in Excel.

6. Select the chart type you want, and then click Next. Excel displays the third ChartWizard dialog box, which shows the predefined formats available for the selected chart type.

7. Select the format you want for your chart by pointing to it.

8. Select the Next button to continue. Excel displays the fourth ChartWizard dialog box, which lists the assumptions ChartWizard makes about how you want your worksheet data displayed in a chart. If any of these assumptions are incorrect, you can change them with the option buttons on the dialog box:

    - If the data series occupy columns in your worksheet rather than the usual rows, choose Columns under Data Series.
    - If the first row of your worksheet contains data rather than labels, choose First Data Series under Use First Row For.
    - If the first column of your worksheet contains data rather than labels, choose First Data Point under Use First Column For.

9. Select the Next command button to display the fifth and final ChartWizard dialog box.

10. If you don't want the ChartWizard to include a legend on your chart, mark the No button.

11. Use the Chart Title text box to give the chart a title.

12. Optionally, use the Axis Titles Category and Axis Titles Value text boxes to give the horizontal and vertical axes titles.

13. To complete the process, select the OK command button at the bottom of the ChartWizard's fifth dialog box. Excel places the completed chart on your worksheet.

See Also Lesson 6

## CLEARING DATA

**MENU PATH** Edit ➤ Clear

The Clear command erases the contents, formats, or notes of selected cells. To use the Clear command, follow these steps:

1. Choose the Clear command from the Edit or Shortcuts menu to display the Clear dialog box.

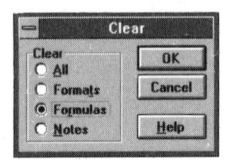

2. Mark the Formulas button to erase cell contents, Formats to erase cell formats, Notes to erase cell notes, or All to erase everything.

## CLOSING A FILE

**MENU PATH** File ➤ Close

**SHORTCUTS** Ctrl-F4 (closes the active document window), Shift-F4 (closes all document windows)

The File menu's Close command closes the active document window. If the active window hasn't been saved, Excel asks whether you want to save the file.

**NOTE** To close all the document windows, press the Shift key and the Shortcut key F4. When you press the Shift key, Excel also changes the Close command on the File menu to the Close All command.

**See Also** Saving Files

# COLOR PALETTE

**MENU PATH** Options ➤ Color Palette

The Option menu's Color Palette command lets you choose a set of colors to use for the Excel document windows. When you choose this command, Excel displays the Color Palette dialog box.

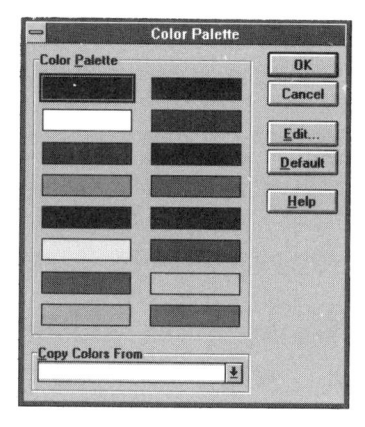

To change one of the colors, double-click on its button, and when Excel displays the Color Picker dialog box, choose the new color you want.

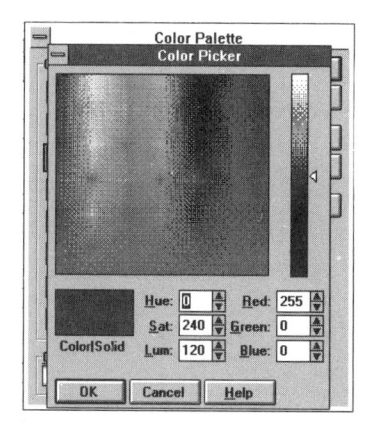

♦ COLUMN WIDTH

You can indicate a color by picking it from the Color Picker's color spectrum chart (specifying its hue, saturation, and luminescence) or by specifying the amount of red, green, or blue in the color.

**See Also** Document Windows

# COLUMN WIDTH

**MENU PATH** Format ➤ Column Width

The Column Width command lets you widen, narrow, or hide and redisplay columns. To use the Column Width command, follow these steps:

1. Select the column or columns you want to change.
2. Choose the Column Width command from the Format menu to display the Column Width dialog box.

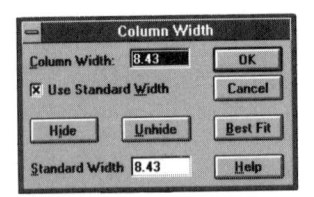

3. Enter the desired width in characters in the Column Width text box. To reset the column width to the default dimension (8.43 characters), mark the Use Standard Width check box. To adjust the column width to hold the widest label or value, select the Best Fit command button. To hide a column, select the Hide command button.

**NOTE** A hidden column is shown as a bold line between letters on the column border. To unhide a column, select a range that includes the columns to the left and right of the hidden column. Choose the Column Width command to display the Column Width dialog box, and then select the Unhide command button.

**See Also** Formatting, Row Height

# CONSOLIDATING DATA

**MENU PATH** Data ➤ Consolidate

The Data menu's Consolidate command lets you combine and summarize data from more than one range and more than one worksheet into a single range on a single worksheet.

**NOTE** For more information on the Consolidate command, refer to your *Microsoft Excel User Guide*.

# COPYING DATA TO THE CLIPBOARD

**MENU PATH** Edit ➤ Copy

**SHORTCUTS** Ctrl-C, Copy tool

The Copy command duplicates the data in a selected worksheet range and temporarily stores it in the Windows Clipboard. It is usually used in combination with the Paste command to duplicate data in other locations. To use the Copy command, first select the worksheet range containing the data you want to duplicate, and then choose the Copy command from the Edit menu or the Shortcuts menu.

**See Also** Cutting Data to the Clipboard, Pasting Data from the Clipboard

# CREATING A NEW FILE

**MENU PATH** File ➤ New

**SHORTCUTS** Shift-F11, Alt-Shift-F1, New Worksheet tool (open new worksheets); F11, Alt-F1 (open new charts); Ctrl-F11, Alt-Ctrl-F1 (open new macro sheets)

The New command creates and opens a new worksheet, macro sheet, chart, workbook, or slides file. To use the New command, follow these steps:

1. Choose the New command from the File menu, or select the New Worksheet tool from the toolbar to display the New dialog box.

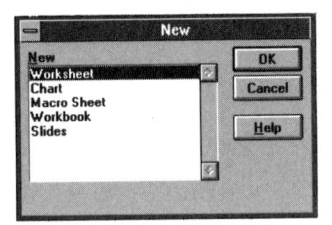

2. Choose Worksheet, Chart, Macro Sheet, Workbook, or Slides from the list box, and select OK to display the new file.

**NOTE** When you create a new chart file, Excel uses the data in the selected range of the active worksheet to create a chart.

**See Also** Charting, Opening a File, Saving a File

# CUTTING DATA TO THE CLIPBOARD

**MENU PATH** Edit ➤ Cut

**SHORTCUTS** Ctrl-X, Shift-Delete

The Cut command removes data in a selected worksheet range and stores it temporarily in the Windows Clipboard. The Cut command is usually used in combination with the Edit menu's Paste command to remove data and place it in another location. First select the worksheet range you want to remove, and then choose the Cut command from either the Edit or the Shortcuts menu.

**See Also** Copying Data to the Clipboard, Pasting Data from the Clipboard

# DATABASES

Although it's not as powerful as specialized, relational database applications, Excel's Data menu offers a convenient means of creating and maintaining simple, one-file databases to organize information. Lesson 8 provides a tutorial on the use of Excel as a database manager.

## TO USE A FORM FOR DATA ENTRY

### MENU PATH  Data ➤ Form

The Form command creates a dialog box for entering data into a database and editing database information. The dialog box includes text boxes for each of the database fields, as well as several command buttons that make data entry easier.

To use the command, you need to have previously defined a database using the Data menu's Set Database command.

## TO FIND DATABASE RECORDS

### MENU PATH  Data ➤ Find

The Find command moves the cell selector to database records that match designated search criteria. The database records must be within a database you've defined using the Set Database command, and the search criteria must have already been specified using the Set Criteria command.

**NOTE**  After you've selected the Find command, scrolling moves the cell selector only to database records that match the search criteria. To turn off the Find mode, choose the Data menu's Exit Find command, which replaces the Find command when Find is activated.

## TO SET A DATABASE RANGE

### MENU PATH  Data ➤ Set Database

The Set Database command identifies the worksheet range where database field names and records are stored. To create a database with the Set Database command, enter your database records in a worksheet using the Data menu's Form command, select the range that contains your database records, and then choose the Set Database command from the Data menu.

**NOTE**  The first row or column of a selected database range should contain the database field names, and the selected range must also include at least one other row or column even if that row or column is blank.

## TO SET SEARCH CRITERIA

### MENU PATH  Data ➤ Set Criteria

The Set Criteria command on the Data menu is used to identify the worksheet range where you entered the search criteria required for the Data menu's Find, Extract, and Delete commands. To use the command, enter your search criteria in a worksheet, select the range containing the criteria, and then choose the Set Criteria command.

## TO SET AN EXTRACTION RANGE

### MENU PATH  Data ➤ Set Extract

The Set Extract command lets you identify the worksheet range into which extracted records are pasted. To use the command, select the worksheet range where you want to paste the extracted records, and then choose the Set Extract command.

**NOTE**  The first row of the extraction range should contain the database field names of the record fields you want pasted.

## TO EXTRACT A DATABASE RECORD

### MENU PATH  Data ➤ Extract

The Extract command copies database records that match designated search criteria. The database records must be within a database you've defined using the Set Database command, and the search criteria must have already been specified using the Set Criteria command. The range to which the copied records are to be pasted must also have been specified using the Set Extract command.

## TO DELETE A DATABASE RECORD

### MENU PATH  Data ➤ Delete

The Data menu's Delete command removes database records that match designated search criteria. The records must be within a database you've defined using the Set Database command, and the search criteria must have already been specified using the Set Criteria command.

# DELETING COLUMNS AND ROWS

### MENU PATH  Edit ➤ Delete

### SHORTCUT  Ctrl-(Hyphen key)

The Delete command lets you delete selected cells or entire columns and rows. Choose the Delete command from either the Edit menu or the Shortcuts menu to display the Delete dialog box. Mark the appropriate option buttons and then select OK.

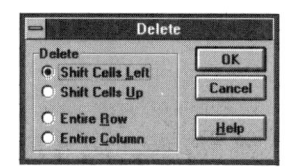

◆ DELETING A FILE

The Shift Cells Left button moves the cells on the right of the deleted cells to the left. The Shift Cells Up button moves the cells below the deleted cells up. You can also delete an entire row or column in which there are selected cells, by marking the Entire Row or Entire Column buttons.

**NOTE** You can also delete entire rows or columns by selecting the row number or column letter in the worksheet border, and then choosing the Delete command.

# DELETING A FILE

**MENU PATH** File ➤ Delete

The File menu's Delete command erases files stored on disk. To use the File Delete command, follow these steps:

1. Choose the Delete command from the File menu to display the Delete Document dialog box.

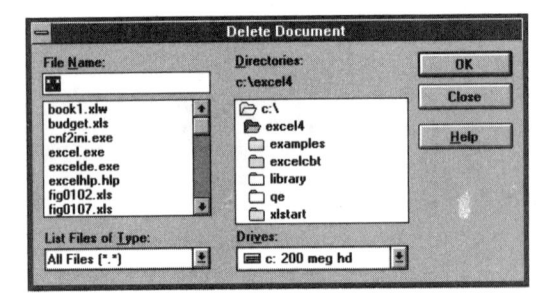

2. Move the selection cursor to the Drives list box, and specify the disk where the file you want is stored.

3. Move the selection cursor to the Directories list box, and specify in which directory the file is stored.

4. Move the selection cursor to the File Name text box and enter the file name, or select the file from the File Name list box.

5. Select OK to complete the process.

# DOCUMENT WINDOWS

Document windows are the windows an application uses to display the files it creates. Excel, for example, displays worksheets, charts, and macro sheets in document windows that appear inside the Excel application window.

## TO ARRANGE SIZE AND POSITION

**MENU PATH** Window ➤ Arrange

The Window menu's Arrange command resizes and moves the open document windows so they can all be viewed as tiles in the Excel application window. The Arrange command also lets you specify whether the window showing a copy of a document should be synchronized to move as you scroll the window that shows the original document.

**NOTE** If you've minimized all the document windows, Excel replaces the Arrange command with the Arrange Icons command. This command neatly arranges the document window icons along the bottom edge of the Excel application window.

## TO CONTROL THE DISPLAY OF DOCUMENT WINDOWS

**MENU PATH** Options ➤ Display

The Display command lets you control how Excel displays document windows. When you choose this command, Excel displays the Display Options dialog box.

◆ DOCUMENT WINDOWS

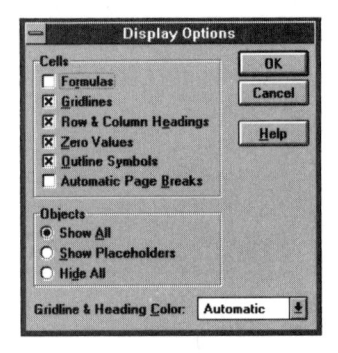

Use the Cells checkboxes to specify whether cells should show formulas (rather than formula results), gridlines, row and column headings, calculated zero values, outline symbols, and automatic page breaks. The Objects buttons specify whether Excel should display embedded objects, show placeholders to identify the object's location, or hide all objects. The Gridline & Heading Color list allows you to specify color for gridlines, row numbers, and column letters.

## TO HIDE A DOCUMENT WINDOW

### MENU PATH  Window ➤ Hide

The Hide command hides the active document so it is not visible in the application window. This command is usually employed to hide windows that need to be open but that you don't need to display, such as macro sheets.

## TO UNHIDE A DOCUMENT WINDOW

### MENU PATH  Window ➤ Unhide

The Unhide command displays a dialog box listing hidden windows. To unhide a previously hidden window, simply select it from the list.

## TO CREATE A NEW DOCUMENT WINDOW

**MENU PATH** Window ➤ New Window

The New Window command creates another document window in the active window. If you've constructed a large worksheet and want to view different parts of the worksheet at the same time, you can use the New Window command to create the additional windows.

## TO VIEW DOCUMENT WINDOW FORMATS

**MENU PATH** Window ➤ View

The View command lets you create different views of a window. A view includes things like print settings, row and column widths, display settings, and even window size.

## TO ZOOM IN AND OUT

**MENU PATH** Window ➤ Zoom

The Zoom command lets you magnify or reduce the size of the document displayed in the active window. When you select this command, Excel displays the Zoom dialog box.

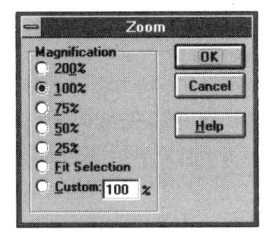

To change the size of a document, select a Magnification option button. If you select the Custom radio button, enter the desired percentage in the text box.

♦ DRAWING FEATURES

## TO SPLIT A WINDOW INTO PANES

**MENU PATH**  Window ➤ Split

The Split command breaks windows into two or four pieces, called panes. Because one window pane can be scrolled independently of the others, the Split command makes it possible for you to view different portions of the same worksheet.

**NOTE**  If the active document is split, the Window menu displays the Remove Split command.

You can adjust the size of each pane by dragging the split bars that separate each pane.

## TO FREEZE PANES ON SPLIT DOCUMENT WINDOWS

**MENU PATH**  Window ➤ Freeze Panes

The Freeze Panes command lets you freeze the top pane, the left pane, or both the top and left panes of a split window so the panes can't be scrolled.

**NOTE**  The Unfreeze Panes command replaces the Freeze Panes command when it has been activated.

**See Also**  Application Windows, Color Palette, Files, Windows

# DRAWING FEATURES

**SHORTCUTS**  Draw box tool, Draw line tool, Drawing toolbar tools

The Draw box and Draw line tools, which are described in Lesson 4, let you draw borders around or lines under worksheet ranges. You can also use the tools on the Drawing toolbar to create lines and shapes.

To display the Drawing toolbar, use the Options menu's Toolbar command. To draw a line or shape using a Drawing tool, select a tool with an icon like the line or shape you want to draw.

**See Also**  Formatting, Graphic Objects, Toolbar Control

◆ EXITING EXCEL

# EXITING EXCEL

**MENU PATH** File ➤ Exit

**SHORTCUT** Alt-F4

The Exit command stops the Excel application program. This command is equivalent to closing the Excel application window by choosing the Close command from the Application window's control menu. If you haven't saved the open worksheet files since the last changes were made, Excel prompts you to save them before exiting.

**See Also** Saving Files

# FILES

Excel stores things like the worksheets, macros, and charts you create in files located on a disk. To identify a file's type, Excel uses the following DOS filename extensions:

| | |
|---|---|
| XLA | add-in files |
| XLC | chart files |
| XLM | macro sheet files |
| XLS | worksheet files |
| XLT | template files |
| XLW | workbook files |

**See Also** Charting, Closing a File, Creating a New File, Deleting a File, Linking Files, Opening a File, Saving a File, Workbooks

# FILLING CELL DATA INTO SELECTED RANGES

**MENU PATH** Edit ➤ Fill Right/Fill Down

**SHORTCUTS** Ctrl-R, Ctrl-D

The Fill Right and Fill Down commands copy labels, values, or formulas, and then fill the cells in a selected range with the copied data. The Fill Left and Fill Up commands replace Fill Right and Fill Down on the Edit menu when you press the Shift key.

To use the Fill commands, first select the worksheet range that includes the data you want copied and the cells you want to fill. Choose the Fill Right or Fill Down command, or press Shift and choose Fill Left or Fill Up to complete the process.

◆ FINDING CELL DATA

# FINDING CELL DATA

**MENU PATH** Formula ➤ Find

**SHORTCUT** Shift-F5

The Find command lets you search through worksheets and macro sheets for specific labels, values, formulas, or formula results. To use the Find command, follow these steps:

1. Select the worksheet range you want to search. Excel searches your entire worksheet if you don't select a specific range.

2. Choose the Find command from the Formula menu to display the Find dialog box.

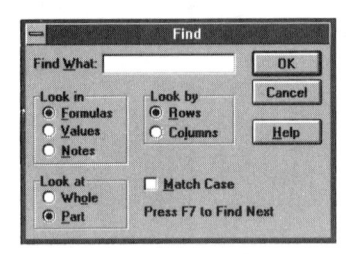

3. Enter the label, value, formula, or formula result you want to find in the Find What text box.

4. Use the Look In option buttons to tell Excel where to search.

5. Use the Look At option buttons to tell Excel whether it must find whole, or exact, matches or can partly match a cell's contents.

6. Use the Look By option buttons to specify a search by row or column.

7. The Match Case check box tells Excel to exactly match the case of the Find What entry.

**NOTE** If Excel finds a label, value, formula, or formula result that matches the search description you entered using the Find dialog box, it moves the cell selector to that cell. To repeat the search, press the Find function key, F7.

**See Also** Cell Characteristics, Replacing Cell Data

# FONT STYLES

**MENU PATH** Format ➤ Font

**SHORTCUTS** Bold tool, Italic tool, Next size larger tool, Next size smaller tool

The Font command lets you change the default font style from 10 point Helvetica. To use the Font command, follow these steps:

1. Select the range where you want to change the font style, and then choose the Font command from either the Format menu or the Shortcuts menu to display the Font dialog box.

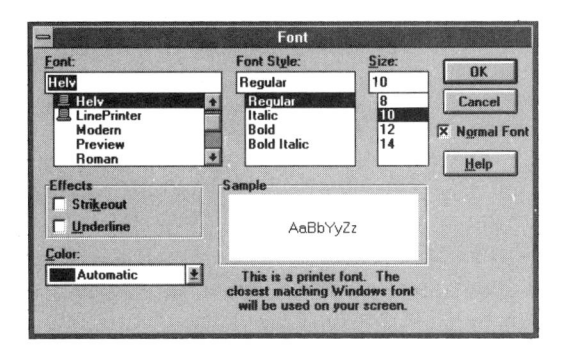

2. Select the font name from the Fonts list box.
3. Select the desired style (Regular, Italic, Bold, etc.) from the Font Style list box.
4. Change the font point size with the Size list box.
5. The Strikeout check box draws a line through the characters in the selected range.
6. The Underline check box underlines the selected characters.

◆ FORMATTING

7. To use a color other than black, activate the Color list and choose the desired color.

**NOTE** The Sample text box displays an example of the current font selection. The Normal Font check box returns the selections to the default settings.

# FORMATTING

Excel's Format menu commands let you change the way your worksheets look. You can do things such as change label and value alignment, add border lines and shading, and specify font styles and sizes.

## TO ALIGN VALUES AND LABELS

**MENU PATH** Format ➤ Alignment

**SHORTCUTS** Left align tool, Center align tool, Right align tool, Center across tool

The Alignment command controls how values and labels are vertically and horizontally aligned in cells, and also how they are oriented. You can also align labels and values with the tools provided on the Excel toolbar. To use the Alignment command, first select the worksheet range that you want to align, and then follow these steps:

1. Choose the Alignment command from either the Format or Shortcuts menu to display the Alignment dialog box.

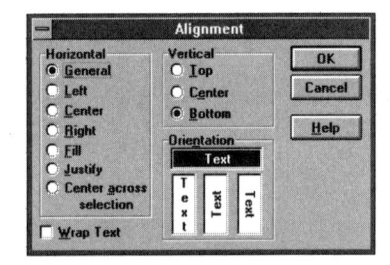

2. Use the Horizontal option buttons (General, Left, Center, Right, Fill, Justify, and Center Across Selection) to control horizontal alignment within cells.

   - General, the default setting, causes values to be right-justified and labels to be left-justified.
   - Left causes both values and labels to be left-justified.
   - Center causes both values and labels to be centered in cells.
   - Right causes both values and labels to be right-justified.
   - Fill repeats a label or value as many times as it will fit in a cell.
   - Justify both left- and right-justifies text within a cell and automatically resizes the row containing the selected cell to accommodate the justified text within the cell.
   - Center Across Selection centers a label or value across the width of the selected range.

3. Use the Vertical option buttons (Top, Center, and Bottom) to vertically align labels and values in cells.

   - Top causes labels and values to be top-justified so they are positioned flush against the top edge of the cell.
   - Center causes labels and values to be centered between the top and bottom edges of the cell.
   - Bottom causes labels and values to be bottom-justified so they are positioned flush against the bottom edge of the cell.

4. The Wrap Text check box justifies text in a cell and also automatically adjusts row height to accommodate the wrapped text within the cell.

5. The Orientation command buttons rotate labels and values.

**NOTE** You may need to adjust the height of rows in the selected range so the rotated text can be read in the worksheet.

# TO JUSTIFY TEXT

**MENU PATH** Format ➤ Justify

♦ FORMATTING

The Justify command breaks a long text label entered into a single cell into several shorter text labels that fill several cells. To use the Justify command, select a worksheet range where the upper left corner of the range contains the cell with the long text label.

The range width should also equal the length desired for the new shortened text labels, and include as many rows as you want new labels. Choose the Justify command to complete the process.

## TO USE AUTOFORMAT

**MENU PATH** Format ➤ AutoFormat

**SHORTCUT** AutoFormat tool

The Format menu's AutoFormat command allows you to simultaneously perform a series of formatting tasks such as value formatting, label and value alignment, font style changes, and so forth. To use the AutoFormat feature, follow these steps:

1. Select the worksheet range you want to format.
2. Choose the AutoFormat command to display the AutoFormat dialog box.

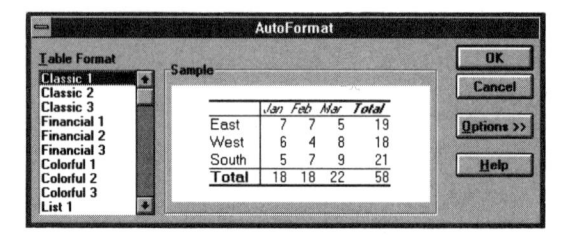

3. From the Table Format list box, select one of the sets of formatting rules. Refer to the Sample box to see how a table formatted according to the selected set of table formatting rules appears.

**NOTE** To apply your selected AutoFormat style to another range on your worksheet, use the AutoFormat tool on the toolbar.

# TO FORMAT BORDERS AND CELLS

**MENU PATH** Format ➤ Border

**SHORTCUTS** Draw box tool, Draw line tool

The Border command lets you draw lines around cells and worksheet ranges, and also shade cells and draw lines. To use the command, follow these steps:

1. Select the worksheet range you want to draw on or shade.
2. Choose the Border command from either the Format menu or the Shortcuts menu to display the Border dialog box.

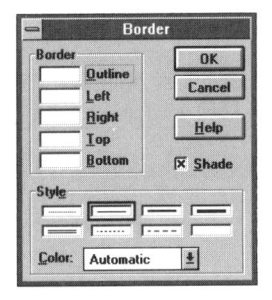

3. To tell Excel where to draw a line, use the Border option buttons.
   - Mark the Outline button to draw a line around the outside edge of the selected worksheet range.
   - Mark the Left, Right, Top, or Bottom buttons to draw a line along a specific edge of the selected range.
4. To shade the cells in the selected range, mark the Shade check box.
5. To describe the type of line you want drawn, use the Style buttons.
6. To choose a color other than black, activate the Color drop-down list box.

◆ FORMATTING

## TO FORMAT NUMBERS

**MENU PATH** Format ➤ Number

The Number command formats values in the selected worksheet range. Formatted values use punctuation such as commas, percent symbols, parentheses, and dollar signs to make values easier to read. To use the Number command, select the worksheet range you want to format, and then follow these steps:

1. Choose the Number command from either the Format or the Shortcuts menu to display the Number Format dialog box.

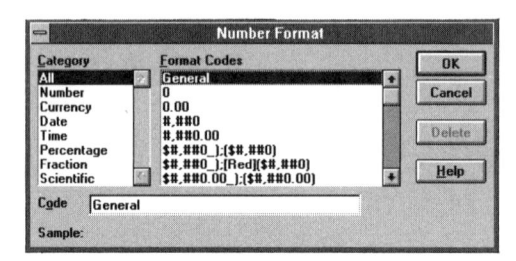

2. Select a format category and style from the Category and Format Codes list boxes.

3. Select OK to complete the process.

**NOTE** Refer to the Sample text box at the bottom of the dialog box to view an example of your format code selection.

## TO APPLY PATTERNS AND CELL SHADING

**MENU PATH** Format ➤ Patterns

The Patterns command gives you control over how cells are shaded, including the colors used for shading foregrounds and backgrounds, and also the patterns used, such as diagonal lines, cross-hatching, and dots. To use the Patterns command, follow these steps:

1. Select the cell or worksheet range you want to shade.
2. Choose the Patterns command from the Format menu or the Shortcuts menu to display the Patterns dialog box.

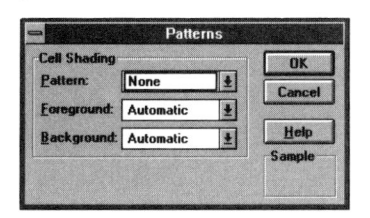

3. Activate the Pattern drop-down list box and select the pattern you want to use for shading.
4. Activate the Foreground drop-down list box and select the color you want to use for the shading pattern.
5. Activate the Background drop-down list box and select the color you want to use as a background behind the shading pattern.

## TO APPLY A STYLE

**MENU PATH** Format ➤ Style

**SHORTCUTS** Style box tool, Paste formats tool

The Style command lets you define formatting styles. A formatting style is a set of formatting rules, including number, font, alignment, border, patterns, and cell protection formatting. To define a new formatting style, choose the Style command. Excel displays a dialog box that allows you to specify a set of formatting rules and name them as a style.

To use a named format style, select the worksheet range where you want the style applied, and then select the style from the Style box on the toolbar.

**See Also** Drawing Features, Font Styles

# FORMULAS

Excel allows you to enter formulas into worksheet cells, and then it calculates the formulas. Formulas can use values, as in =2+2. Or, they can refer to cells either by using cell addresses, as in =A1+A2, or by using range names, as in =LABOR+OVERHEAD.

**See Also** Calculating Worksheets, Labels, Values

# GOTO COMMAND

**MENU PATH** Formula ➤ Goto

**SHORTCUT** F5

The Goto command moves the cell selector to a specified cell without scrolling through your worksheet. The Goto command can also move the cell selector to the upper-left corner of a named range.

Choose the Goto command from the Formula menu or press F5 to display the Goto dialog box.

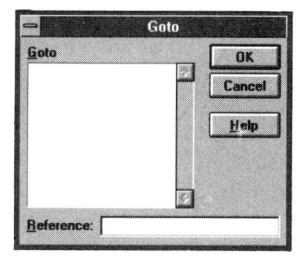

Enter the address of the cell you want to go to in the Reference text box. To move the cell selector to the upper-left corner of a named range, select the range from the Goto list box.

**NOTE** To have items listed in the Goto list box, you must first create named ranges on your worksheet. Refer to Lesson 3 for a tutorial on naming and working with ranges.

**See Also** Range Names

# GRAPHIC OBJECTS

Excel lets you add graphic objects to your worksheets. One way you can create these graphic objects is using the Drawing toolbar, in which case you create objects such

◆ GRAPHIC OBJECTS

as arrows, lines, and boxes. The more usual way you will create these graphic objects, however, is with the ChartWizard. The chart that the ChartWizard embeds in a worksheet is a graphic object.

## GROUPING GRAPHIC OBJECTS

### MENU PATH  Format ➤ Group

The Group command creates one graphic object by grouping other selected graphic objects. The Group command makes it easier to move and resize more than one object at a time.

To use the Group command, first select each of the graphic objects to be included in the new group by holding down the Ctrl key and then clicking on each of the objects. Choose the Group command to complete the process.

**NOTE**  The Ungroup command is displayed on the Format menu when a selected object was created using the Group command.

## TO INSERT OBJECTS IN DOCUMENTS

### MENU PATH  Edit ➤ Insert Object

The Insert Object command lets you embed objects such as charts, worksheets, or macro sheets in open Excel documents. When you choose this command, Excel displays the Insert Object dialog box.

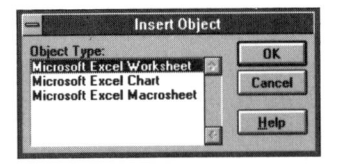

Simply select the object you want to insert from the Object Type list, and then select OK to complete the process.

# TO MOVE OBJECTS BACK AND FRONT

**MENU PATH**  Format ➤ Send to Back/Bring to Front

Graphic objects normally appear on a worksheet in the order in which you create or modify them, with the most recent object at the front. The Send to Back and Bring to Front commands let you change that order to work with any object. Send to Back moves the selected object to the back; Bring to Front brings it forward. Select the object you want to move, and choose the appropriate command.

**SHORTCUT**  Send to Back and Bring to Front tools (drawing toolbar)

# TO CONTROL OBJECT PROPERTIES

**MENU PATH**  Format ➤ Object Properties

The Object Properties command lets you control how graphic objects are connected to worksheets and how these objects change when the cells they are connected to change. To use the command, follow these steps:

1. Select the object for which you want to change properties.
2. Choose the Object Properties command to display the Object Properties dialog box.

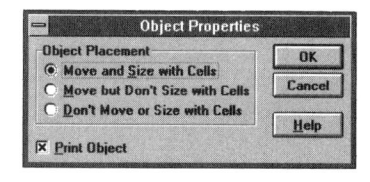

3. Mark the appropriate option buttons to control the object's properties when its associated cells are moved.
4. To print the object when the worksheet to which it's connected prints, mark the Print Object checkbox.
5. Select OK to complete the process.

**See Also** Charting, Drawing Features

# GROUPING WORKSHEETS AND MACRO SHEETS

**MENU PATH** Options ➤ Group Edit

The Group Edit command lets you group worksheets and macro sheets so that subsequent commands and changes applied to one worksheet affect the entire group.

**See Also** Macros

# HELP

Excel's Help system incorporates the standard Windows Help features and a few extra items: help systems designed for 1-2-3 and Multiplan users, and information about product support.

## HELP ON EXCEL

**MENU PATH** Help ➤ Contents/Search

The Help menu's Contents command starts the Windows Help application and displays a list of general help topics.

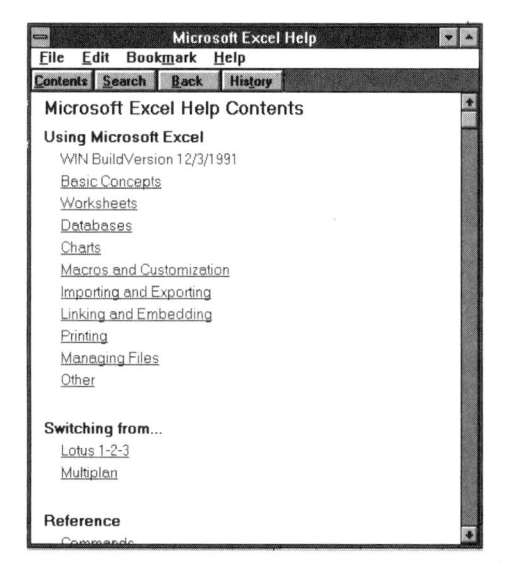

To see specific listings within a category, click on the topic name. To get help information on a specific topic, click on it.

The Search command starts the Windows Help application and displays the Search dialog box.

◆ HELP

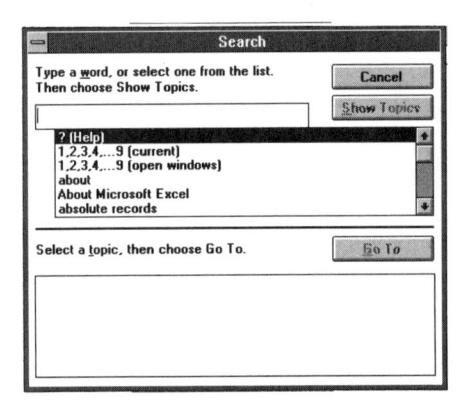

Enter the topic you want to search for in the text box, and then select the general and specific categories Excel displays in the list boxes.

**NOTE** Help topics are identified with a special color, usually green, on the Help application windows, and when you point to a help topic in text, Windows changes the mouse pointer to a hand.

You can also choose the Search command by selecting the Search button on the Help Contents window.

## HELP FOR LOTUS 1-2-3 USERS

**MENU PATH** Help ➤ Lotus 1-2-3

The Lotus 1-2-3 Help command makes it easier for former Lotus 1-2-3 users to use Excel. It lets you choose a Lotus 1-2-3 command, such as Worksheet Insert Row, and then view the equivalent Excel command performed step-by-step.

## HELP FOR MICROSOFT MULTIPLAN USERS

**MENU PATH** Help ➤ Multiplan Help

The Multiplan Help command makes it easier for former Microsoft Multiplan users to begin using Excel. When you choose a Multiplan command, the equivalent Excel command is executed step-by-step so you can see how Excel works.

## PRODUCT SUPPORT

**MENU PATH**  Help ➤ Product Support

The Product Support command starts the Windows Help application and shows the Microsoft product support available for Excel.

**See Also**  On-Line Demonstration and Tutorial Programs

◆ IMPORTING AND EXPORTING DATA

# IMPORTING AND EXPORTING DATA

Excel can import data files created by other applications, to be used in Excel worksheets; it can also export worksheets for use by other applications. When you import data, you may need to parse it into appropriate worksheet columns.

## TO EXPORT DATA TO ANOTHER APPLICATION

MENU PATH  File ➤ Save As

1. In the Save As dialog box, first select the file to be exported.
2. In the Save File as Type list box, choose the appropriate file type for the other application.
3. Verify the file name extension (e.g., .doc if you're exporting to Word) in the File Name text box and click OK.

## TO IMPORT DATA FROM ANOTHER APPLICATION

MENU PATH  File ➤ Open

1. In the Open dialog box, first select the correct file type from the List Files of Type list box.
2. Choose the correct drive and directory path.
3. Select the file from the File list box and click OK.

## TO PARSE IMPORTED TEXT

MENU PATH  Data ➤ Parse

When you import columnar data from a non-spreadsheet application, it may be in text form, with spaces rather than tabs separating the fields (columns). Excel reads all such data into a single worksheet column. Use the Parse command to divide ("parse") the fields into the appropriate columns in your worksheet. You can parse one row or several rows.

**See Also** Opening a File, Saving a File

# INSERTING COLUMNS AND ROWS

**MENU PATH** Edit ➤ Insert

**SHORTCUT** Ctrl-Shift-+

The Insert command lets you insert columns and rows in a worksheet. To insert entire rows or columns, select the row number above where you want a new row inserted or the column letter to the left of where you want a new column inserted. To insert cells in rows or columns, select a number of cells above or to the left of where you want the same number of new cells inserted, and then choose the Insert command to display the Insert dialog box.

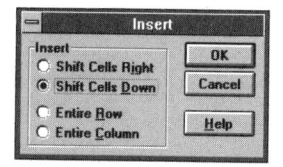

Use the Shift Cells Right and Shift Cells Down buttons to tell Excel how to adjust your worksheet to fit the newly inserted cells. Select OK to complete the process.

**NOTE** You can also insert entire rows or columns with the Entire Row or Entire Column option buttons.

## LABELS

Excels allows you to enter pieces of text you don't want to manipulate arithmetically into worksheet cells. Excel calls these pieces of text *labels*. Typically, you use labels to describe and document the values stored in worksheet cells.

**See Also** Formulas, Values

## LINKING FILES

**MENU PATH** File ➤ Links

The Links command displays a dialog box that lists the files linked by formulas to the active file. You can also use the Links command to change the files linked to the active file, open files that are linked to the active file, and retrieve values from the files linked to the active file.

**See Also** Pasting Link Formulas

# MACROS

Excel lets you create separate programs, called *macros*, to automate repetitive or complex keystroke or command sequences. Macros, then, let you use the Excel program as a platform upon which to build other applications, such as point-of-sale or inventory management systems. See Lesson 7 for a detailed tutorial on recording and running macros.

## TO RECORD A MACRO

### MENU PATH  Macro ➤ Record

The Record command lets you create a macro by recording the actions you want to automate. To use the Record command, follow these steps:

1. Choose the Record command from the Macro menu to display the Record Macro dialog box.

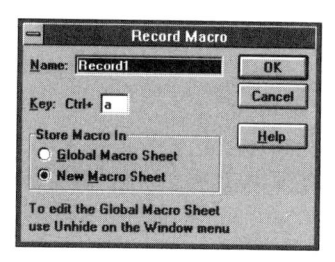

2. In the Name text box, enter a name for the macro.
3. In the Key box, enter the key that when combined with the Ctrl key makes up the alternate shortcut key for running your macro.
4. Use the Store Macro In buttons to tell Excel to store your macro in the Global Macro Sheet or in a separate, New Macro Sheet.
5. Perform the actions you want your macro to perform.
6. When you are finished, choose the Stop Recorder command.

◆ MACROS

## TO START AND STOP THE RECORDER

**MENU PATH** Macro ➤ Start Recorder/Stop Recorder

The Macro menu's Start and Stop Recorder commands let you stop and then resume a macro recording session. Once a macro session is started, the Start command changes to the Stop Recorder command.

**NOTE** The Stop and Start Recorder commands can be very useful when there are actions you need to perform but don't want recorded in your macro.

## TO RESUME RECORDING

**MENU PATH** Macro ➤ Resume

The Macro menu's Resume command restarts a macro you suspended using the Pause button on the Single Step dialog box.

## TO ASSIGN A MACRO TO AN OBJECT

**MENU PATH** Macro ➤ Assign to Object

The Assign To Object command lets you connect a macro to a worksheet or macro sheet object. After the connection is made, clicking on the object starts the macro.

**NOTE** To identify objects with macro connections, Excel changes the mouse pointer to a hand whenever the pointer is on a connected object.

## TO RUN A MACRO

**MENU PATH** Macro ➤ Run Macro

**SHORTCUT**  Ctrl + key combination (assigned when recording the macro)

To use the Run command, select it from Macro menu and display the Run Macro dialog box.

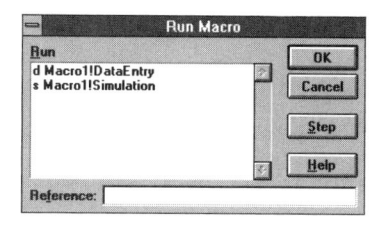

Select the macro you want to run from the list box, and then select OK.

**NOTE**  Macros in the GLOBAL.XLM macro sheet are always available. Macros in separate macro sheets are available only when those macro sheets are open.

The Step command button on the Run Macro dialog box displays the Single Step dialog box. This feature lets you run your macros step-by-step.

# MACRO SET RECORDER

**MENU PATH**  Macro ➤ Set Recorder

The Macro menu's Set Recorder command lets you specify where in the active macro sheet a macro created by the Recorder should be placed. To use this command, first display the macro sheet in which the recorded macro should be placed. Next, select the first cell of the macro sheet range into which the macro should be placed. Then choose the Set Recorder command.

# RELATIVE AND ABSOLUTE RECORDING

**MENU PATH**  Macro ➤ Relative Record/Absolute Record

The Relative Record and Absolute Record commands let you specify whether your macro records cell selector movements in relative or absolute terms. Excel assumes

◆ MODELING

absolute references for cell selector movement and displays the Relative Record command as an option. When you choose the Relative Record command, Excel replaces it with the Absolute Record command.

**NOTE** When you record cell selector movements in absolute terms, they are treated as if you simply used the Formula menu's Goto command. The Relative Record command lets you record all the actions performed to move the cell selector from one place to another.

# MODELING

Excel provides three quantitative modeling tools, which let you go beyond what's possible with just spreadsheet formulas and functions: the Scenario Manager command, which performs what-if analysis; the Goal Seek command, which performs target-value modeling; and the Solver command, which performs linear and nonlinear optimization modeling.

## OPTIMIZATION MODELING

**MENU PATH** Formula ➤ Solver

The Solver command lets you perform linear and nonlinear programming. Linear and nonlinear programming solve problems in which an optimization function is maximized or minimized, subject to certain specified constraints.

To comfortably use the Solver command and safely rely on its results, you should understand optimization problem solving. Refer to your *Microsoft Excel User Guide* for more information on the mechanics of the Solver command.

## TARGET VALUE MODELING

**MENU PATH** Formula ➤ Goal Seek

The Goal Seek command lets you solve target value models to find the single input value that causes a dependent formula to return a desired target value. To use the Goal Seek command, follow these steps:

1. Build a worksheet model with the formula you want to return a specific target value in one cell, and the formula input that returns the target value in another cell.

2. Choose the Goal Seek command from the Formula menu to display the Goal Seek dialog box.

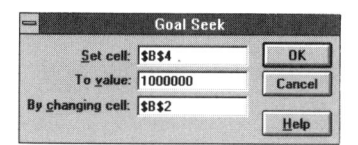

3. Enter the formula cell address in the Set cell text box.
4. Enter the target value in the To value text box.
5. Enter the input value cell address in the By changing cell text box.
6. Select the OK command button to initiate the target value calculations, and Excel displays the Goal Seek Status dialog box.

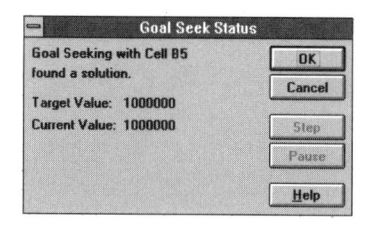

7. Select one of the following command buttons to complete the process.

   - OK closes the dialog box and places the value that causes the formula to return the target value in the input cell.
   - Cancel closes the dialog box without changing the input cell value.
   - Step incrementally steps through the target value calculations, one input value at a time.

◆ MODELING

- Pause temporarily suspends target value calculation. To restart calculation, select the Continue button.

## WHAT-IF MODELING

**MENU PATH** Formula ➤ Scenario Manager

The Scenario Manager command performs what-if analysis, which lets you experiment with changing formula results as one or more input values change. To use the Scenario Manager, follow these steps:

1. Build a worksheet model including the output value formula in one cell, and the variable input value in another cell.
2. Choose the Scenario Manager command from the Formula menu to display the Scenario Manager dialog box.

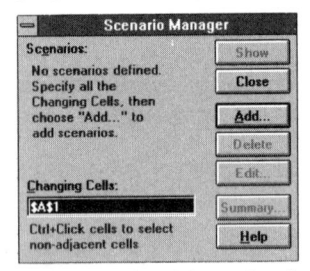

3. Enter a cell address for the variable input value in the Changing Cells text box.
4. To add input value scenarios, choose the Add button, and Excel displays the Add Scenario dialog box.

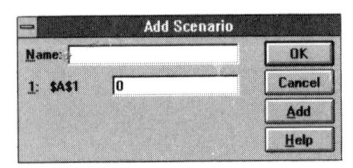

5. Enter a name for the scenario in the Name text box.
6. Enter the input value for the first scenario in the other text box, and select OK to return to the Scenario Manager dialog box.

**MODELING** ◆

7. To initiate a scenario, select it from the Scenarios list box, and then select the Show command button.

8. To create a scenario summary worksheet, select the Summary command button to display the Scenario Summary dialog box.

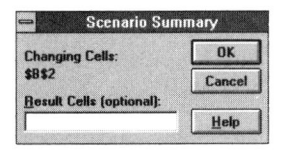

```
┌─ Scenario Summary ─────────┐
│ Changing Cells:    [ OK ]  │
│ $B$2              [Cancel] │
│ Result Cells (optional):   │
│ [            ]    [ Help ] │
└────────────────────────────┘
```

9. Enter the cell address of the output formula in the Result Cells text box. To test more than one output formula, enter each cell address in the text box, separating them with commas.

10. To create a summary worksheet, select OK.

**NOTE** To delete or edit a scenario, choose the Scenario Manager command and select the scenario from the list. To delete the scenario, select Delete. To edit the scenario by changing either the name or the input value, select Edit, and then make the needed changes using the Edit Scenario dialog box.

**157**

# OBJECT LINKING AND EMBEDDING

Windows 3.1 and higher provide a handy feature for sharing data between Excel and other Windows applications, called Object Linking and Embedding, or OLE. You can use OLE, for example, to put an Excel worksheet or chart in a Word for Windows document.

To use OLE, you simply copy the data from one application's source document and paste it into another application's destination document. When you paste the data into the destination document, Windows gives you the choice of either embedding the data or of linking the data in the source and destination documents. If you embed the data, you've only copied the data. If you link the copied data, however, Windows will update the destination document for changes to the source document. Lesson 9 provides a tutorial on object linking and embedding.

**See Also** Copying Data to the Clipboard, Pasting Data from the Clipboard

# ON-LINE DEMONSTRATION AND TUTORIAL PROGRAMS

Excel offers new users both a set of demonstration programs, called Introducing Microsoft Excel, and a tutorial, called Learning Microsoft Excel.

## TO RUN THE EXCEL DEMONSTRATIONS

**MENU PATH** Help ➤ Introducing Microsoft Excel

The Introducing Microsoft Excel command displays a screen that lets you choose one of three interactive product demonstrations.

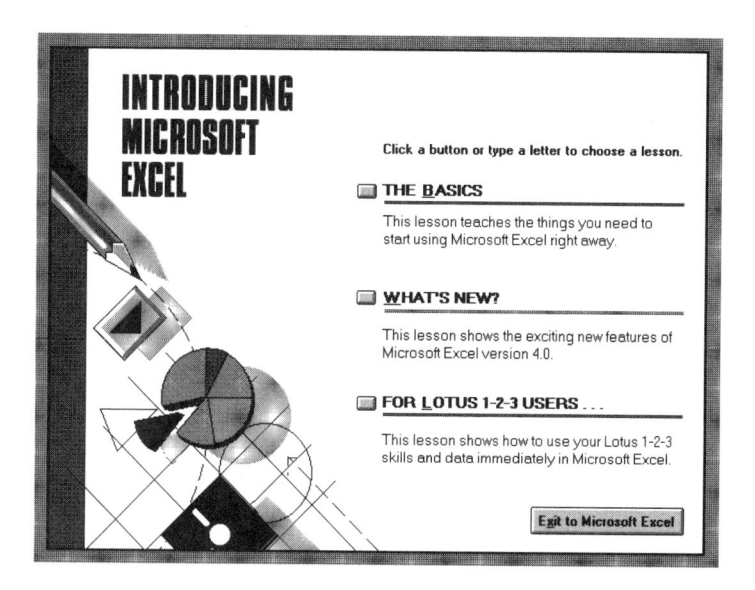

The demonstrations include an overview of the basic mechanics of the Excel program, a summary of new features for version 4.0, and an orientation for former Lotus 1-2-3 users. You can select the button to activate a demonstration, or choose the Exit to Microsoft Excel command button.

## TO RUN THE EXCEL TUTORIAL

**MENU PATH** Help ➤ Learning Microsoft Excel

The Learning Microsoft Excel command starts an interactive tutorial that teaches basic Excel skills, including explanations of how to construct worksheets, create charts, build databases, write macros, and use toolbars.

**See Also** Help

## OPENING A FILE

**MENU PATH** File ➤ Open

◆ OUTLINING WORKSHEET DATA

**SHORTCUTS** Ctrl-F12, Open file tool

The Open command lets you retrieve files saved on disk. To use the Open command, follow these steps:

1. Choose the Open command from the File menu or use the Open file tool on the tool bar to display the File Open dialog box.

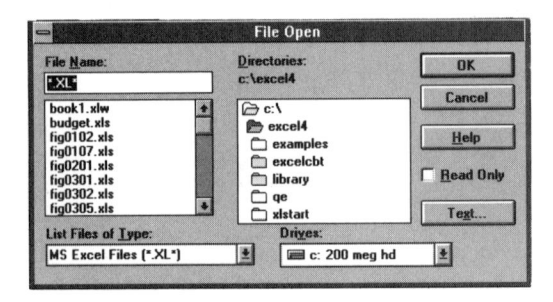

2. Move the selection cursor to the Drives list box, and specify the disk that contains your file.

3. Move the selection cursor to the Directories list box, and specify the appropriate directory.

4. Enter the file's name in the text box or select the file from the File Name list box.

5. Select OK to complete the process.

**NOTE** To retrieve files you only want to read but not modify or save as another version, mark the Read Only check box.

**See Also** Creating a New File

# OUTLINING WORKSHEET DATA

**MENU PATH** Formula ➤ Outline

The Formula Outline command lets you compress your worksheet data into outline form, so that only summary rows and columns are visible. To outline your worksheet, first select the worksheet range you want outlined, choose the Outline command, and then select the Create button from the dialog box.

**NOTE** For more information on outlining, refer to *Mastering Excel 4 for Windows*, by Carl Townsend (SYBEX, 1992).

◆ PAGE SETUP

# PAGE BREAKS

**MENU PATH** Options ➤ Set Page Break

The Set Page Break command lets you set page breaks for printing. To specify a horizontal page break, select the row above where the page break should occur. For a vertical page break, select the column to the left of where the page should break. When you've selected the appropriate row or column, choose the Set Page Break command from the Options menu.

**NOTE** If a page break has been set at the selected row or column, Excel displays the Remove Page Break command.

**See Also** Page Setup, Printing

# PAGE SETUP

**MENU PATH** File ➤ Page Setup

The Page Setup command lets you specify a wide variety appearance, orientation, and scaling options for your printed pages. To use the Page Setup command, follow these steps:

1. Choose the Page Setup command from the File menu to display the Page Setup dialog box.

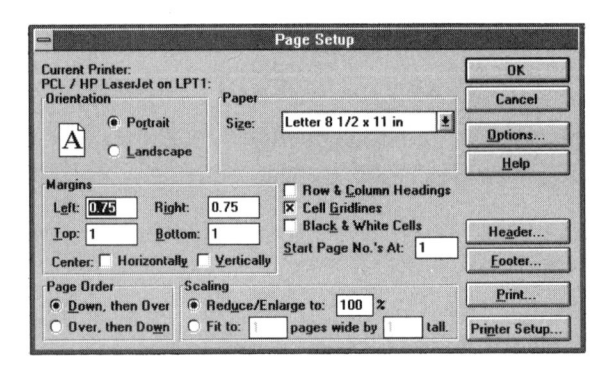

2. Enter, mark, and select the appropriate setup options on the dialog box, and then select OK to complete the process.

**NOTE** The Page Order option buttons break a worksheet into columns or rows so the worksheet prints down and then over by columns, or over and then down by rows.

To enlarge or reduce a document to fit on a certain number of pages, use the Fit To text boxes.

**See Also** Page Breaks, Printing

# PASTING DATA FROM THE CLIPBOARD

When you've copied data to the Clipboard, you can paste either all of it, or only selected parts of it, into an Excel worksheet (or another Windows application).

## TO PASTE ALL CLIPBOARD DATA

**MENU PATH** Edit ➤ Paste

**SHORTCUT** Shift-Ins

The Paste command on the Edit and Shortcuts menus copies data currently stored in the Windows Clipboard to selected locations on worksheets or charts. Use the Paste command after you have used the Cut or Copy commands to move or copy data to the Clipboard.

To use the Paste command, first select the worksheet or chart location where you want to paste the Clipboard data, and then choose the Paste command.

## TO PASTE ONLY SELECTED CLIPBOARD DATA

**MENU PATH** Edit ➤ Paste Special

♦ **PASTING FUNCTIONS IN FORMULAS**

The Paste Special command copies only specified data from the Clipboard. Follow these steps, after using the Copy or Cut commands, to paste selected data from the Clipboard:

1. Choose the Edit menu's Paste Special command to display the Paste Special dialog box.

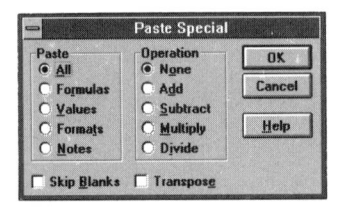

2. Use the option buttons to indicate the data you want to copy.

3. To skip pasting blanks from the Clipboard to the selected location on your worksheet, mark the Skip Blanks checkbox.

4. To transpose a range as you paste it, making rows into columns or columns into rows, mark the Transpose checkbox.

5. To combine the values you're pasting from the Clipboard with the values in the destination range to perform an arithmetic operation, use the Operation buttons.

**NOTE** When you use the Paste Special command on data copied to the Clipboard by another application, Excel displays a modified version of the dialog box.

If you use the Paste Special command while working with charts, Excel displays a dialog box that asks how the data should be interpreted.

**See Also** Copying Data to the Clipboard, Cutting Data to the Clipboard

# PASTING FUNCTIONS IN FORMULAS

**MENU PATH** Formula ➤ Paste Function

**SHORTCUT** Shift-F3

The Paste Function command makes it easier to work with worksheet and macro sheet functions by allowing you to paste function names and arguments into formulas you're creating or editing. To use the Paste Function command, follow these steps:

1. Position the insertion point at the exact location where you want the function inserted.
2. Choose the Paste Function command from the Formula menu to display the Paste Function dialog box.

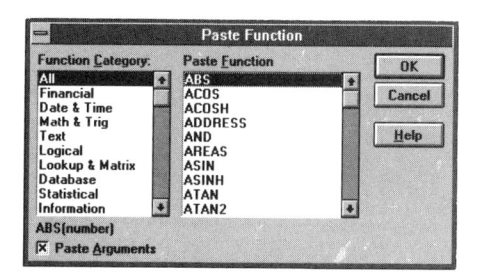

3. Select a category from the Function Category list, and then choose a function from the Paste Function list box.

**NOTE** To have Excel include one-word descriptions of a function's arguments, mark the Paste Arguments checkbox.

# PASTING LINK FORMULAS

**MENU PATH** Edit ➤ Paste Link

The Edit menu's Paste Link command creates a link formula between two Excel documents. If you copy the contents of cell A1 in the worksheet named BUDGET.XLS and paste, using the Paste Link command, those contents to cell B2 in the worksheet named EXPENSES.XLS, Excel creates the link formula =BUDGET!A1 in cell B2 of EXPENSES.XLS.

♦ PRINTING

See Also  Copying Data to the Clipboard, Linking Files

# PRINTING

Excel offers a variety of printing and print-preview features.

## TO PRINT A WORKSHEET

**MENU PATH** File ➤ Print

**SHORTCUTS** Ctrl-Shift-F12, Print tool

The Print command prints the worksheet, chart, or macro sheet in the active window. To use the Print command, follow these steps:

1. Choose the Print command from the File menu or the Print tool from the tool bar to display the Print dialog box.

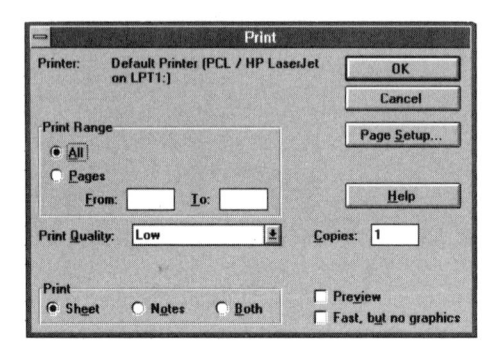

2. Use the Print Range options to designate the number of pages you want to print.

3. The Print Quality list box lets you select a print quality supported by your printer.

4. The Print option buttons let you print just a worksheet, the notes attached to the cells in a worksheet, or both.
5. Enter the number of copies you want to print.
6. To display your document in the Print Preview window before printing it, mark the Preview check box.

**NOTE** The Page Setup command button activates the Page Setup dialog box, which lets you specify a variety of appearance, orientation, and scaling options for your printed pages.

## TO PREVIEW A PRINTOUT

**MENU PATH** File ➤ Print Preview

The Print Preview command displays a window showing what each of your pages should look like printed.

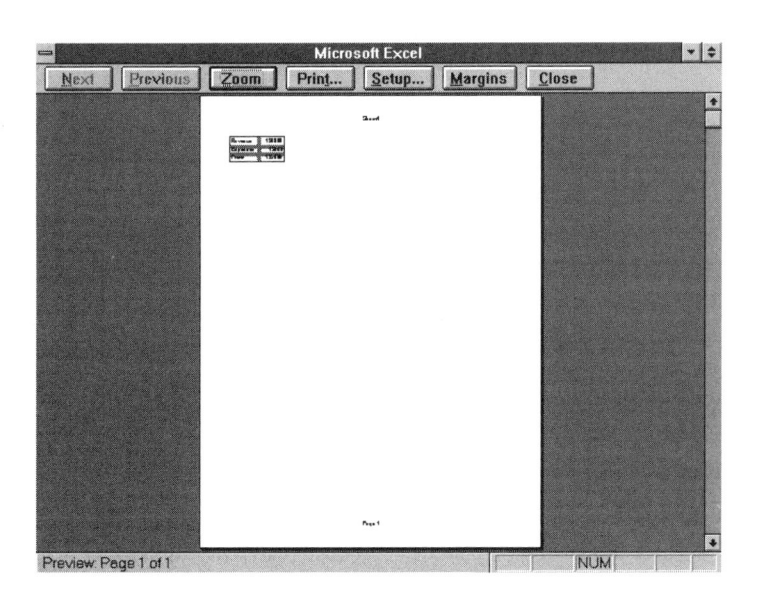

♦ TO PRINT PREDEFINED REPORTS

To view other pages in a document, use the Next and Previous buttons. To magnify a page, use the Zoom button. To print the document, use the Print button. You can also use the Setup and Margins command buttons to change the way the page is printed. To remove the Print Preview window from your display, select the Close command button.

# TO PRINT PREDEFINED REPORTS

**MENU PATH** File ➤ Print Report

The Print Report command allows you to print, create, edit, and delete predefined reports. A report definition consists of a view, or set of print settings (defined with the Window ➤ View command), and a scenario created by the Formula menu's Scenario Manager command (see Modeling).

## TO SET PRINT AREAS

**MENU PATH** Options ➤ Set Print Area

The Set Print Area command lets you specify one or more worksheet ranges for printing. To use the Set Print Area command, select the worksheet range or ranges you want to print, and then choose the Set Print Area command from the Options menu. Excel names the selected range *Print Area* and then prints that named range when you choose the Print command from the File menu or use the Print tool.

**NOTE** Unless you set a print area, Excel prints your entire worksheet when you use the Print command.

## TO SET PRINT TITLES

**MENU PATH** Options ➤ Set Print Titles

The Set Print Titles command lets you specify selected rows or columns to be printed as borders on each document page. To use the Set Print Titles command, follow these steps:

1. Choose the Set Print Titles command from the Options menu to display the Set Print Titles dialog box.

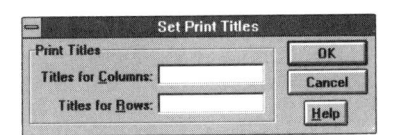

2. Enter the address of the rows or columns you want to use as borders in the appropriate text boxes.

3. Select OK to complete the process.

**NOTE** Specify the column or row address as absolute. For example, to use rows 1 and 2 as a horizontal border, enter $1:$2.

**See Also** Formatting, Modeling, Page Breaks, Page Setup

# Q+E APPLICATION

Q+E is a separate application that lets you work with databases. Using Q+E, you can access and update database files created by many popular database applications, including dBASE files, SQL Server files, Oracle files, and even Microsoft Excel files if they have a defined database.

**NOTE** For more information on the Q+E application, refer to your *Q+E for Microsoft Excel User Guide*.

# RANGE NAMES

Once you've named a worksheet range, you can use its name in commands and formulas rather than its cell address. For example, if the worksheet range A1:A50 is named COSTS, the two function formulas SUM(A1:A50) and SUM(COSTS) are equivalent.

## TO NAME A RANGE

**MENU PATH** Formula ➤ Define Name

**SHORTCUT** Ctrl-F3

To use the Define Name command, follow these steps:

1. Select the range you want to name.
2. Choose the Define Name command from the Formula menu to display the Define Names dialog box.

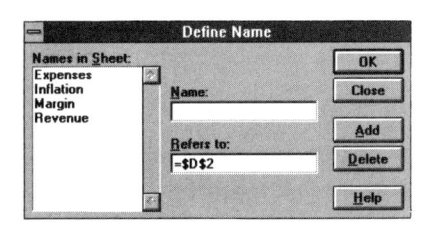

3. Enter the range name in the Name text box.
4. Verify the range definition shown in the Refers to text box.
5. Choose the Add command to define additional names, and select OK to complete the process.

**NOTE** You can also delete selected range names using the Delete button on the Define Names dialog box.

◆ RANGE NAMES

## TO APPLY A RANGE NAME

**MENU PATH** Formula ➤ Apply Names

The Apply Names command lets you apply range names to range references in a selected area of a worksheet. This command can be useful when you want to update existing formulas with new range names. To use the Apply Names command, follow these steps:

1. Select the worksheet area where you want Excel to apply range names.
2. Choose the Apply Names command to display the Apply Names dialog box.

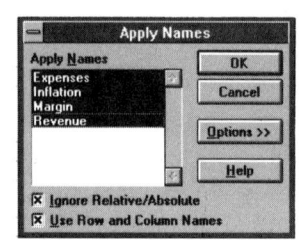

3. The names you want to apply to range references can be selected from the Apply Names list box. To select more than one range name, hold down Ctrl while you click on additional names.
4. Mark or unmark the Ignore Relative/Absolute checkbox as desired.
5. If you unmark the Use Row and Column Names checkbox, select OK to complete the process.
6. If you mark the Use Row and Column Names checkbox, select the Options command button to display additional boxes and buttons for specifying how Excel should construct range name equivalents.

## TO CREATE A RANGE NAME FROM A WORKSHEET LABEL

**MENU PATH** Formula ➤ Create Names

**172**

**SHORTCUT** Ctrl-Shift-F3

The Create Names command lets you define range names using worksheet labels adjacent to the ranges you want to name. To use the Create Names command, follow these steps:

1. Select the worksheet range that includes both the labels to be used as range names and the range you want to name.
2. Choose the Create Names command from the Formula menu to display the Create Names dialog box.

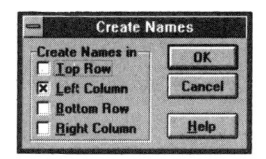

3. Mark the appropriate checkbox to locate the labels you want to use as a range name.
4. Select OK to complete the process.

**NOTE** Excel won't use values as range names. If you use the Create Names command to designate a date value as a range name, Excel converts it to a text label.

# TO PASTE A RANGE NAME

**MENU PATH** Formula ➤ Paste Name

**SHORTCUT** F3

The Paste Name command makes it easier to enter range names into formulas you're creating or editing. To use the Paste Name command, follow these steps:

1. Position the insertion point at the exact location the range name should be inserted.

2. Choose the Paste Names command from the Formula menu to display the Paste Name dialog box. The Paste Name list box shows all the range names in the active sheet.

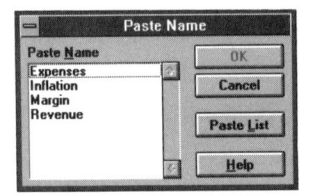

3. Select the name you want to insert in the currently selected cell, and select OK to complete the process.

**NOTE**  If the formula bar isn't active, Excel activates it and enters an equal sign (=) before pasting the name.

The Paste List button on the Paste Name dialog box allows you to paste a two-column list of names and range definitions in a selected area of your worksheet. Move the selection cursor to the worksheet location where you want to paste the list, and then use the Paste Name command Paste List button to complete the operation.

# REPEATING THE LAST COMMAND

**MENU PATH**  Edit ➤ Repeat

**SHORTCUT**  Alt-Enter

The Repeat command simply repeats the last command chosen. Excel continually updates the name of the Repeat command to reflect the last selected command.

**NOTE**  If you've just pasted something using the Edit menu's Paste command, the Repeat command appears as Repeat Paste.

# REPLACING CELL DATA

**MENU PATH** Formula ➤ Replace

The Replace command lets you search through worksheet and macro sheet cells for specific labels, values, formulas, or pieces of formulas, and then replace them. To use the Replace command, follow these steps:

1. Select the worksheet range you want to search.
2. Choose the Replace command from the Formula menu to display the Replace dialog box.

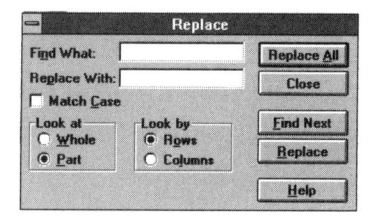

3. Enter the label, value, formula, or formula fragment you want to search for in the Find What text box.
4. Enter the label, value, formula, or formula fragment you want to substitute in the Replace With text box.
5. Use the Look At option buttons to tell Excel to match a cell's contents exactly or partly.
6. Use the Look By option buttons to tell Excel to search by rows or columns.
7. The Match Case check box tells Excel to search only for instances of the text in the Find What box that exactly match its case (capitalization).
8. Select the Replace All, Find Next, or Replace command buttons to initiate the search.

**NOTE** The Replace All button replaces all occurrences. The Find Next and Replace command buttons let you individually locate and replace occurrences. To terminate the Replace operation, select the Close command button.

**175**

◆ ROW HEIGHT

**See Also** Cell Characteristics, Finding Cell Data

# ROW HEIGHT

**MENU PATH** Format ➤ Row Height

The Row Height command lets you increase or decrease the height of any row; it also lets you hide or redisplay rows. To use the command, follow these steps:

1. Select the row or rows you want to change.
2. Choose the Row Height command from either the Format menu or the Shortcuts menu to display the Row Height dialog box.

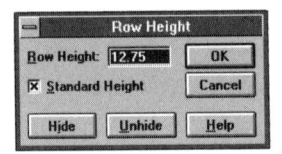

3. Enter the desired row height in points in the Row Height text box, and then select OK to complete the process.

**NOTE** To reset row height to the default dimension (12.75 points), mark the Standard Height check box.

To hide a row, select the Hide command button. To unhide a row, select a range that includes the rows both above and below the hidden row, choose the Row Height command, and select the Unhide command button from the dialog box.

# Saving a File

**MENU PATH**  File ➤ Save/Save As

**SHORTCUTS**  Shift+F12 (Save), F12 (Save As), Save File tool

The File menu's Save command saves files that have already been named and assigned a disk storage location. If a file hasn't already been assigned a name and storage location and you choose the Save command or select the Save File tool, Excel executes the Save As command.

Use the Save As command to name and save files that haven't previously been saved, or to copy them to a different location or in a different file format. To use the Save As command, follow these steps:

1. Choose the Save As command from the File menu or select the Save file tool from the toolbar. Excel displays the File Save As dialog box.

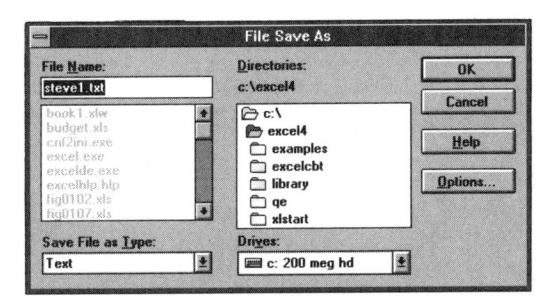

2. Use the Drives list box to specify the disk where you want to store the file.
3. The Directories list box lets you specify the directory.
4. To save the file in a format other than Excel, activate the Save File As Type list box and select the appropriate file format.
5. Use the File Name text box to enter a valid DOS filename (Excel adds a 3-letter extension for you) and click OK.

**NOTE** If you select the Options command button on the File Save As dialog box, Excel lets you create backup copies of files, add passwords, and create read-only files.

## TO SAVE A FILE IN A WORKBOOK

**MENU PATH** File ➤ Save Workbook

The Save Workbook command lets you save worksheets, macros and charts in a single file called a workbook. If you later open a workbook, Excel opens each item in the workbook file. To use the Save Workbook command, follow these steps:

1. Choose the Save Workbook command from the File menu to display the File Save As dialog box.
2. Use the Drives, Directories, and File Name boxes to enter a valid DOS filename and specify the disk and directory locations for your file. Excel adds an .XLW file extension for you.

**NOTE** When a workbook file is open, Excel lists a workbook contents window showing each file in the group. You can use this window to add and remove files.

**See Also** Creating a New File, Opening a File, Security, Workbooks

# SECURITY

Excel provides various methods of securing, or protecting, the worksheets you create: file-level password protection, file read-only status, and document or cell protection.

## PASSWORD PROTECTION

**MENU PATH** File ➤ Save As

Excel lets you assign passwords to the files you create. Once a password has been assigned, Excel requires anyone opening the file to supply the password. To assign passwords, you use the Options command button on the File Save As dialog box. The File Save Options dialog box, which Excel displays if you select the Options command button, includes a text box you can use to assign a password.

## READ-ONLY STATUS

### MENU PATH  File ➤ Save As

Excel allows you to mark files as read-only, which means they can't be modified or deleted. To mark a file as read-only, you use the Options command button on the File Save As dialog box. The File Save Options dialog box, which Excel displays if you select the Options command button, includes a check box you can mark to open files as read-only.

## PROTECTING DOCUMENTS

### MENU PATH  Options ➤ Protect Document

The Protect Document command turns on cell-level, object-level, and window-level document protection. When you select the Protect Document command, Excel displays the Protect Document dialog box.

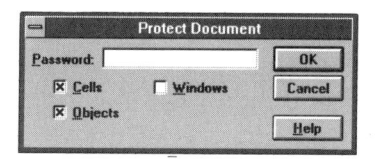

You can specify the type of document protection and a password for disabling document protection. With cell-level protection, cells marked as locked can't be modified and cells marked as hidden can't have their contents viewed on the formula bar. Object-level protection prevents objects embedded in documents from being modified. Window-level protection keeps windows from being modified.

◆ SECURITY

**NOTE** The Unprotect Document command appears on the Options menu when document protection is enabled. If a password was entered when document protection was turned on, the Unprotect Document command displays a dialog box to collect the password.

## CELL PROTECTION

**MENU PATH** Format ➤ Cell Protection

The Cell Protection command works with the Options menu's Protect Document command to let you identify cells that can't be modified and can't have their contents viewed on the formula bar once document protection has been activated. To use the Cell Protection command, follow these steps:

1. Select the worksheet range containing the cells you want to protect.
2. Choose the Cell Protection command from the Format menu to display the Cell Protection dialog box.

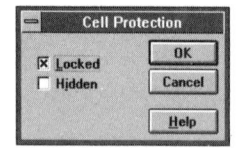

3. To protect cells in the selected worksheet range from having their contents modified once the Protect Document command is chosen, mark the Locked checkbox.
4. To prevent cells in the selected worksheet range from having their contents viewed on the formula bar once the Protect Document command is chosen, mark the Hidden checkbox.

**See Also** Saving a File

# SERIES VALUES

**MENU PATH** Data ➤ Series

The Series command enters a series of values into a selected range of a worksheet. You can use the Series command to enter values that increase or decrease arithmetically or exponentially. You can also use the Series command to enter date values that increase or decrease by units of time.

To use the command, enter the starting value for the series in one cell, and select the range including the starting value and each of the other cells you want filled. Choose the Series command from the Data menu to display the Series dialog box. Make your selections on the dialog box, and then select OK to complete the process.

**See Also** Filling Cell Data into Selected Ranges

# SHOWING THE ACTIVE CELL

**MENU PATH** Formula ➤ Show Active Cell

The Show Active Cell command moves the sheet displayed in the active window so that the active cell is visible. The active cell is the cell with the cell selector.

# SORTING WORKSHEET DATA

**MENU PATH** Data ➤ Sort

The Data menu's Sort command lets you sort, or organize, any group of worksheet cells or database records. To use the Sort command, follow these steps:

1. Select the range holding the cells or database records you want to sort.
2. Choose the Sort command to display the Sort dialog box.

♦ SPELL-CHECKING DOCUMENTS

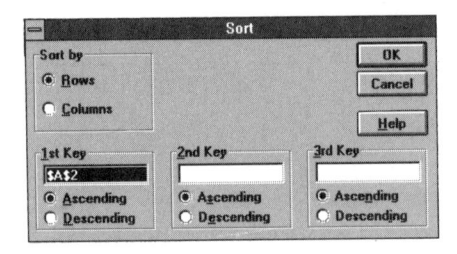

3. Mark the Rows or Columns option button to choose a method for sorting your selected range.

4. Select the 1st Key for sorting by entering the address, as an absolute reference, of the cell that contains the label, value, or database field you want to sort by.

5. Mark the Ascending or Descending option buttons to tell Excel how to sort your data.

6. Specify 2nd and 3rd Key settings to accommodate labels, values, or database fields that may be identical to previously selected keys.

**See Also** Databases

# SPELL-CHECKING DOCUMENTS

**MENU PATH** Options ➤ Spelling

The Spelling command checks the spelling of words on the formula bar or in a selected worksheet range. To use the Spelling command, follow these steps:

1. Select the cells whose labels and notes you want to check for misspelled words. If you want to check the spelling of words on the formula bar, select the words in the formula you want to check. Excel checks all the words in the active worksheet if you do not make a specific selection.

2. Choose the Spelling command from the Options menu.

3. When Excel finds a word not in its dictionary, it displays the word in the Spelling dialog box.

**SPELL-CHECKING DOCUMENTS** ◆

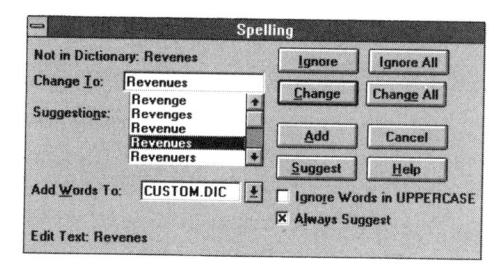

**4.** Type a replacement word in the Change To text box, select one of the suggested spellings from the Suggestions list, or use the Ignore command button if you're satisfied with the current spelling.

**5.** Select the Change button to change the identified word to a new spelling you've designated.

**NOTE** For a detailed tutorial on the Spelling command, refer to Lesson 3.

**183**

# TABLE COMMAND SCENARIOS

**MENU PATH** Data ➤ Table

The Table command lets you quickly perform "what-if" analysis with one or two input values. To use the Table command, first build a worksheet model including the formula and the series of input values you want to recalculate. The Table command performs a what-if analysis that recalculates the formula for each of the input values.

**See Also** Modeling

# TOOLBAR CONTROL

**MENU PATH** Options ➤ Toolbars

The Toolbars command lets you control whether Excel displays a toolbar beneath the menu bar. It also lets you display different toolbars for outlining, charting, and so on. You can even create new toolbars and customize existing ones by adding and removing command buttons.

# UNDOING MISTAKES

**MENU PATH** Edit ➤ Undo

**SHORTCUTS** Ctrl-Z, Alt-Backspace

The Undo command reverses the effect of most data entry and worksheet editing actions. To use the command, simply choose it from the Edit menu after you've done something you wish you hadn't.

**NOTE** After you choose the Undo command, Excel displays the Redo command, which restores what you just undid.

## VALUES

Excels allows you to enter numbers you want to manipulate arithmetically into worksheet cells. Excel calls these numbers *values*.

**See Also** Formulas, Labels

# WINDOWS

The word *windows* can refer to several things within the Windows operating environment, which can be somewhat confusing. When capitalized, it always refers to the Windows operating environment software and is a trademark of Microsoft Corporation. Otherwise, it refers either to the application windows that programs like Excel use to display menu bars and document windows or to the document windows that appear inside application windows and show documents like worksheets and charts.

**See Also** Application Windows, Document Windows

# WORKBOOKS

**MENU PATH** File ➤ New

Excel lets you group documents—worksheets, charts, macro sheets, and so forth—together into workbooks. Once you've thus grouped documents, you can save and open the files as a group simply by saving or opening the workbook.

Take the following steps to create a new workbook:

1. Select New from the File menu.
2. Select Workbook from the New list box.
3. You'll see an empty workbook (with the heading "Workbook Contents") in the document window; select Add.
4. Select Open from the Add to Workbook dialog box.
5. You'll see a standard Open File dialog box; select a file and click OK.
6. The file will appear in the workbook. Repeat steps 3–5 to add more files.
7. Close the file and answer "Yes" when asked whether to save it. Excel adds the extension .XLW to whatever name you provide.

**See Also** Opening a File, Saving a File

# Appendix A

# Installation Instructions

Installing Excel 4.0 for Windows isn't difficult, as the setup utility provided with Excel guides you through the procedure with a series of prompts. If you haven't already installed the program, you should do so now, before trying out the lessons in Part I.

*Installation Instructions*
**APPENDIX**

You can use the following step-by-step instructions:

1. Start Windows and display the Windows Program Manager.
2. Insert Excel Disk 1 into drive A.
3. Choose the Run command from the File menu to display the Run dialog box.
4. Type **A:Setup** in the Command Line text box.
5. Press ↵ twice to bypass the two introductory message boxes.
6. Select the type of installation you want from the next message box.
7. By default, your Excel program and data files are installed in C:\EXCEL. When the next message box appears, press ↵ or enter the path for another directory in the text box provided.

> *If the directory where you want Excel installed doesn't already exist, Excel asks if you want it created. Select Yes, and Excel creates the required directory for you.*

8. The next message box asks if you want to enable help for Lotus 1-2-3 users and use Excel with Lotus command styles. Press ↵ to accept the default setting or select Yes to use the Lotus 1-2-3 features.
9. Insert other setup disks as Excel prompts you, and press ↵ to continue.

As Excel copies files to your hard disk, it displays a message box that shows you the progress of the setup operation. When setup is complete, the Microsoft Excel 4.0 program group is added to your Windows Program Manager.

> *When you first start Excel, it displays an introduction screen with command buttons for selecting tutorials on Excel basics, the new features for Excel 4.0, and converting from Lotus 1-2-3. To skip these tutorials select the Exit button.*

# INDEX

**Note:** In this index, **boldface** type indicates the pages where you'll find the primary discussion of an Excel command, dialog box, or operation, or the definition of an important concept. Page numbers in regular type provide further information on these topics. *Italic* type identifies the illustration of an Excel dialog box.

## Symbols

\# (pound sign), as formula error indicator, 18
^ (caret), for exponentiation, 15
$ (dollar sign), as absolute cell reference indicator, 31
\* (asterisk), for multiplication, 15
> (less-than symbol), as comparison operator, 94
= (equal sign)
    as comparison operator, 94
    as formulas indicator, 15
> (greater-than symbol), as comparison operator, 94
– (hyphen or minus sign), for subtraction, 15
/ (slash), for division, 15

## A

absolute cell references, **31**, 114
Absolute Record command, 81, **153–154**
active cell
    changing with Find command, **34**, **94–95**, 121
    changing with Goto command, **6**, 141
    showing, 181
Add-ins command, **109**
addition, 19
aligning labels and values, 40–41, 134–135
Alignment command/dialog box, **40–41**, *41*, 134–135

Analysis Tools, **109**
applications
    running multiple, 98–100
    sharing data between, 102–106
    starting, 99
application windows, **4**, 5, **110–111**
Apply Names command/dialog box, **172**, *172*
Area charts, advantages of, 70
Area chart tool, 68
arguments (function input values), 19, 20
Arrange command, **125**
Arrange Icons command, **125**
arrow keys, for moving cell selector, 6
Arrow tool (chart toolbar), 68, **69**
Assign to Object command, **152**
AutoFormat command/dialog box, **38–40**, *39*, 136
Autosum button, **19**
AVERAGE function, **19**
axes, with titles (on charts), 67

## B

Backspace key, for deletions, 10
backups, automatic, 111
Bar charts, advantages of, 71
Bar chart tool, 68
Border command/dialog box, **45–46**, *46*, 137
borders, formatting, 45–46, 137
Bring to Front/Send to Back commands, **143**

**191**

## C

Calculate Now command, 18
Calculation command, 18, 112
Cancel command, 10
Cascade command, 100
categories, 63
Cell Protection command/dialog box, 180, *180*
cell references, 16–17, 112, 114. *See also* ranges of cells
    absolute versus relative, 30–31
    recording in macros, 81
cells, 5. *See also* ranges of cells
    adding explanatory notes to, 109–110
    addresses of, 112
    deleting, 33, 123
    formatting with patterns and colors, 138–139
    inserting, 32
    protecting, 180
    selecting by specified criteria, 112–114
    shading and borders for, 45–46, 137
    showing active, 181
    sorting, 91–92, 181–182
cell selector, 5
    moving with Find command, 34, 94–95, 121
    moving with Goto command, 6, 141
Center Across Selection tool, 40, 134
centering
    labels, 40
    at print time, 51
Center tool, 40, 134
charts
    embedding in documents, 142
    formatting, 63–67
    grouping into workbooks, 187
    opening, 57
    printing, 76, 166–167
    saving, 75–76
    sharing with other applications, 102
    sizing, 52, 68
    titles and legends for, 66–67
    types and uses of, 68, 69–74
ChartWizard, 62–69, 114–115
ChartWizard dialog boxes, 63, 64–65, 66–67, 66
ChartWizard tool, 68
checking spelling, 35–36, 182–183

Choose File ➤ New command, 56–57
circular references in formulas, 18, 112
Clear command/dialog box, 26, *26*, 116
Clipboard
    for copy and paste operations, 119, 163–164
    for cut and paste operations, 120
    for sharing data between applications, 103
Close All command, 57
Close command, 57, 116
closing active windows, 57
Color Palette command/dialog box, 117–118, *117*
Color Picker dialog box, 117–118, *117*
Column chart, example of, 69
Column charts, advantages of, 72
Column chart tool, 68
columns
    breaking and printing by, 51
    deleting, 33, 123
    formatting, 46–47
    hiding or unhiding, 47, 118
    inserting, 32, 149
Column Width command/dialog box, 47, 118, *118*
Combination charts, advantages of, 74
Combination chart tool, 68
commands, repeating, 174
comparison operators, 94
Consolidate command, 119
Contents/Search command, 145–146
Control ➤ Switch To command, 98
Control menu, 98
Copy command, 28–31, 119
copying
    with fill operations, 32, 131
    formulas, 30–31
    labels and values, 28–30
    and pasting data into other applications, 104, 158
    ranges of cells, 119
Copy tool, 28–31, 119
Create Names command, 172–173
Criteria command/dialog box, 93–94, *94*
Ctrl keys, to start macros, 78, 153
Ctrl-PgUp/PgDn keys, navigating in worksheets with, 6
CUSTOM.DIC dictionary file, 35, 36
cut-and-paste operations, 28–32. *See also* pasting

Cut command, **31**, 119

# D

Data ➤ Consolidate command, **119**
Data ➤ Delete command, **123**
Data ➤ Extract command, **95**, 123
Data ➤ Find command, **94–95**, 121
Data ➤ Form command, **89**, 121
Data ➤ Parse command, **148–149**
Data ➤ Series command, **83–84**, 85, 181
Data ➤ Set Criteria command, **122**
Data ➤ Set Database command, **88**, 122
Data ➤ Set Extract command, **95**, 122
Data ➤ Sort command, **91–92**, 181–182
Data ➤ Table command, **184**
databases, **88-96**
    searching with Find command, **34**, **94–95**, 121
    specifying range for field names and records, 122
data points, **63**
data series, **63**, 181
    choosing rows or columns for, 56, 66
    text in, 67
Data Series dialog box, **84**, 85
Define Name command/dialog box, **20–22**, *21* **171**
Delete command (Data menu), **123**
Delete command/dialog box (Edit menu), **33**, 33, 123–124
Delete command (File menu), **57–58**, 123–124
Delete Document dialog box, *55*, *57*, *124*
Delete key, 10, 26
deleting. *See also* erasing
    active windows, 57
    cells, rows or columns, **33**, 123
    contents of cell ranges, 26
    database records, 91, 123
    files, **57–58**, 123–124
directories
    selecting for Excel, 190
    selecting for file deletions, 58
    selecting for file retrievals, 14
    selecting for macro sheets, 82
    selecting upon file saves, 10
Display command, **125–126**

Display Options dialog box, *126*
#DIV/0 error message, 18
documents, sizing, 127
document windows, **4–5**, *125*
Draw Box/Draw Line tools, **46**, 128–129, 137

# E

Edit ➤ Clear command, **26**, 116
Edit ➤ Copy command, **28–31**, 119
Edit ➤ Cut command, **31**, 119
Edit ➤ Delete command, **33**, 123–124
Edit ➤ Fill Left/Fill Up commands, **32**, 131
Edit ➤ Fill Right/Fill Down commands, **32**, 131
Edit ➤ Insert command, **32**, 149
Edit ➤ Insert Object command, **142**
Edit ➤ Paste command, **28–30**, 163
Edit ➤ Paste Link command, **165**
Edit ➤ Paste Special command, **163–164**
Edit ➤ Redo command, **185**
Edit ➤ Repeat command, **95**, 174
Edit ➤ Undo command, **28**, 185
editing
    database records, 90–91
    formulas, 17, 18
    and Undo command, **28**, 185
embedded objects, **106**, 126, 142
engineering tools, in Analysis Toolpack Add-in, 109
Enter command, to affirm data entries, **10**
entering
    with automatic fill operations, **32**, 131
    chart legends and titles, 66, 67
    database data, 89
    worksheet formulas, 15–18
    worksheet labels, 8
    worksheet values, **9–10**, 181
Enter key, to affirm data entries, 10
erasing. *See also* deleting
    contents of ranges, **26–27**, 116
    data form entries, 89
    files, 57–58
    formulas, **26**, 116
    notes for formulas, **26**, 116
error messages, 18
Esc key, to cancel data entry, 10
Excel. *See also* cells; worksheets

**193**

◆ Index

controlling window (workspace) of, 111
exiting, 11, 130
installing, 190
starting, 4
tutorial, 159
Exit command, 11, 130
exiting
   Excel, 11, 130
   Print Preview window, 54
   search operations, 95, 121
exponential notation, used for numeric overflows, 10
exporting files, 58–59, 148–149
extensions
   .BAK for backups, 111
   .XLA for add-in files, 131
   .XLC for charts, 75, 131
   .XLM for macro sheets, 79, 131
   .XLS for worksheets and databases, 11, 96, 131
   .XLT for template files, 131
   .XLW for workbook files, 131, 178
Extract command, 95, 123

# F

F2, for editing, 10
fields, parsing into worksheet columns, 148–149
File ➤ Close command, 57, 116
File ➤ Delete command, 57–58, 123–124
File ➤ Exit command, 11, 130
File ➤ Links command, 150
File ➤ New command, 119–120, 187
File ➤ Open command/dialog box, 14–15, 58, 59 148, 159–160
File ➤ Page Setup command, 51, 162–163
File ➤ Print command, 50, 100, 166–167
File ➤ Print Preview command, 52–54, 167–168
File ➤ Print Report command, 168
File ➤ Save As command/dialog box, 10–11, 148, 177, 178–179
File ➤ Save Workbook command, 178
filename extensions. *See* extensions
files. *See also* security; worksheets
   deleting (erasing), 57–58, 123–124
   handling multiple, 56–57

importing and exporting, 58–59, 148–149
linking, 150
opening, 159–160
printing to, 50
print spool files, 100
read-only, 178
File Save Options dialog box, 111
Fill Left/Fill Up commands, 32, 131
Fill Right/Fill Down commands, 32, 131
financial tools, in Analysis Toolpack Add-in, 109
Find command (Data menu), 94–95, 121
Find command/dialog box (Formula menu), 34, 34, 132
finding
   database records, 93–95
   with Extract command, 95
   with Find command, 34, 94–95
Find Next button, 35
Font command, 43–44, 133
fonts
   formatting with AutoFormat, 38–40, 136
   styles and sizes for, 43–45
Form ➤ Criteria command, 93–94
Format ➤ Alignment command, 40–41, 134–135
Format ➤ AutoFormat command, 136
Format ➤ Border command, 45–46, 137
Format ➤ Cell Protection command, 180
Format ➤ Column Width command, 47, 118
Format ➤ Font command, 43–44, 133
Format ➤ Group command, 142
Format ➤ Justify command, 135–136
Format ➤ Number command, 42–43, 138
Format ➤ Patterns, 138–139
Format ➤ Row Height command, 46, 47, 176
Format ➤ Send to Back/Bring to Front commands, 143
Format ➤ Style command, 139
Format ➤ Ungroup command, 142
formatting
   with Autoformat command, 38–40, 136
   choosing styles for, 139
   erasing, 26
   files for import or export, 58–59
   font styles and sizes, 43–45
   labels and values, 40–41, 134–135
   numbers, 42–43

with Page Setup command, **51**, 162–163
row and column size, 46–47
values, **40–41**, 138
Form command, **89**, 121
forms, for ease of data entry, **89**, 121
Formula ➤ Apply Names command, **172**
Formula ➤ Create Names command, **172–173**
Formula ➤ Define Name command, **171**
Formula ➤ Find command, **34**, 132
Formula ➤ Goal Seek command, **154–156**
Formula ➤ Goto command, **6**, **7**, 141
Formula ➤ Note command, **109–110**
Formula ➤ Outline command, **160–161**
Formula ➤ Paste Function command, **164–165**
Formula ➤ Paste Names command, **173–174**
Formula ➤ Replace command, **34–35**, 175
Formula ➤ Scenario Manager command, **156–157**
Formula ➤ Select Special command, **112–114**
Formula ➤ Show Active Cell command, **181**
Formula ➤ Solver command, **154**
formula bar, 4, 5
formulas, **140**. *See also* functions
copying, **30–31**
entering, **15–18**
erasing, **26**, 116
finding, 34
linking, 165
moving, 31
pasting functions into, 164–165
replacing, **34–35**, 175
Fourier Analysis tools, in Analysis Toolpack Add-in, 109
Free Text tool, **69**
Freeze Panes command, **128**
functions. *See also* formulas
how to use, 18–20
pasting into formulas, 164–165

# G

GLOBAL.XLM file, 79, 153
Goal Seek command, **154–156**
Goto command/dialog box, **6**, **7**, 23, 141, *141*
graphic objects, 141–143
gridlines, 51, 126
chart tool, 68, **69**

Group command, **142**
Group Edit command, **144**
grouping
graphic objects, 142
worksheets and macro sheets, 144

# H

headers, 52, 126. *See also* titles
Help ➤ Contents/Search command, **145–146**
Help ➤ Introducing Microsoft Excel command, **158–159**
Help ➤ Learning Microsoft Excel command, 159
Help ➤ Lotus 1-2-3 command, **146**, 190
Help ➤ Multiplan Help command, **146–147**
Help ➤ Product Support command, **147**
Help
for Multiplan users, 146–147
starting, 7, **145–146**
for users of Lotus 1-2-3, 146
Hide command, **126**
hiding
columns, **47**, 118
macro sheets, 126
rows, **46–47**, 176
status bar, scroll bars and formulas bars, 111
High-Low chart tool, 68
horizontal gridlines tool, 68

# I

importing, files, **58–59**, 148–149
Insert command/dialog box, **32**, *33* 149
inserting rows, columns or cells, 32
Insert Object command/dialog box, **142**, *142*
installing, Excel, 190
Introducing Microsoft Excel command, **158–159**

# J

Justify command, **135–136**

◆ Index

# K

keys
    for deletions, 10
    for entering values, 9
    navigating in worksheets with, 6
    recording in macros, **78–80**

# L

labels, **150**
    copying, 28–30
    entering, 8
    finding, 34
    formatting, 40–41, 136
    moving, 31
    placing on charts, 66
    repeating with Fill option, 41
    replacing, **34–35**, 175
    spreading over several cells, 135–136
Learning Microsoft Excel command, **159**
Left Align tool, **40**, 134
legends, placing on charts, 66
legend tool, 68, **69**
linear/nonlinear programming, with Solver command, 154
Line charts
    advantages of, 72
    example of, 67
Line chart tool, 68
lines
    formatting for, **45**, 137
    line-drawing tools for, 46
linking
    files, 150
    formulas, 165
    objects, 106, **158**
Links command, **150**
Lotus 1-2-3, help for users of, 146, 190

# M

Macro ➤ Absolute Record command, 81
MAcro ➤ Assign to Object command, **152**
Macro ➤ Record command, **78–80**, 151

Macro ➤ Relative Record/Absolute Record commands, 81, **153–154**
Macro ➤ Resume command, **102**, 152
Macro ➤ Run command, **80**, 152–153
Macro ➤ Set Recorder command, **153**
Macro ➤ Start Recorder/Stop Recorder command, **82**, 152
macros, **77**, 151
    assigning to worksheets or macro sheets, 152
    with commands, 83–86
    keystroke versus command, 78
    opening upon startup of Excel, 109
    pausing recording, 82
    recorder tips, 81–82
    recording commands as, 83–86
    recording keystrokes as, 78–80
    and recording relative cell references, 81
    running, 80–81
macro sheets, **79**, 82
    embedding in documents, 142
    grouping, 144
    grouping into workbooks, 187
    hiding, 126
    opening, 57
    printing, 166–167
    specifying placement of macros in, 153
margins, selecting for printing, **51**, 54
menu bar, **4**, 5
    for charts in windows, 76
modeling, **154**
    by target value, 154–155
    optimization, 154
    what-if, 156–157
mouse pointer
    cross-hair style, 63
    as hand, 146
    as hourglass symbol, 18
    as magnifying glass with zoom feature, 54
Multiplan Help command, **146–147**
multiple applications, running, 98–100
multiple files, handling, 56–57
multitasking, 98–100

# N

naming
    ranges of cells, 23, **171–174**
    worksheets, 11

New command/dialog box, **56–57**, *56*, 119–120, 187
New Window command, **127**
New worksheet tool, **57**
Note command, **109–110**
notes for formulas
    erasing, **26**, 116
    printing, 50
Number command, **42–43**, 138
Number Format dialog box, **42**, *42*, *138*
numbers, formatting, 42–43

## O

Object Properties dialog box, *143*
OLE (object linking and embedding), **102**, 158
Open command, **14–15**, 148, 159–160
Open File tool, **14**
opening
    charts, 57
    databases, 88
    files, **14**, 57, 159–160
    macro sheets, 57
    windows, 57
    workbooks, 57
optimization modeling, **154**
Options ➤ Add-ins command, **109**
Options ➤ Analysis Tools, **109**
Options ➤ Calculation command, **18**, 112
Options ➤ Color Palette, **117–118**
Options ➤ Display command, **125–126**
Options ➤ Group Edit command, **144**
Options ➤ Protect Document command, **179–180**
Options ➤ Remove Page Break command, **56**, 162
Options ➤ Set Page Break command, 55, **56**, 162
Options ➤ Set Print Area command, **54–55**, *55*, 168
Options ➤ Set Print Titles command, **55–56**, *55*, 168–169
Options ➤ Spelling command, **35–36**, 182–183
Options ➤ Toolbars command, **184**
Options ➤ Unprotect Document command, **180**

Options ➤ Workspace command, **111**
orientation, landscape or portrait, 41, 51
Outline command, **160–161**

## P

page breaks
    deleting, 56
    for printed worksheets, 51, 162
Page Setup command/dialog box, **51**, *51*, 162–163
parentheses, 16, 19
Parse command, **148–149**
passwords, adding when saving files, 178
Paste command, **28–30**, 163
Paste Formats tool, **28**, 139
Paste Function command, **164–165**
Paste Link command, **165**
Paste Name command/dialog box, **173–174**, *174*
Paste Special command/dialog box, **163–164**, *164*
pasting
    all Clipboard data, 163
    data into other applications, 104, 158
    range names into formulas, 173–174
    selected Clipboard data, 163–164
Patterns command/dialog box, **138–139**, *139*
Pause command, **102**
pausing
    printer operations, 102
    recording of macros, 82
percentages
    scaling printed pages by, 51
    scaling zoomed documents by, 127
PgUp/PgDn keys, navigating in worksheets with, 6
pictures, **38**
Pie charts, advantages of, 72–73
Pie chart tool, 68
PI function, **19**
point sizes (for fonts), 45
precedence, of operations in formulas, 15–16
Preferred chart tool, 68
Preview command, **52–54**, 167–168
Print command/dialog box, **50**, *50* 100, 166–167

**197**

printers
    changing active, 52
    selecting resolution for printing, 50
    troubleshooting, 100–102
printing
    charts, **76**, 166–167
    to disk files, 50
    macro sheets, **82**, 166–167
    pausing, 102
    previewing, **52–54**, 167–168
    with Print Manager, 100–102
    reports, 168
    worksheets, **50–56**, 166–167
Print Manager, **100–102**, *101*
Print Preview command, **52–54**, 167–168
Print Preview window, **52**, *53*
Print Report command, **168**
Product Support command, **147**
Program Manager window, **99**, *99*
Protect Document command/dialog box, **179–180**, *179*

## Q

Q+E application program, 90, **170**
querying. *See also* finding
    databases, **93–95**

## R

Radar charts, advantages of, 73
Radar chart tool, 68
ranges of cells. *See also* cell references
    consolidating and reusing data from, 119
    copying, 119
    erasing contents of, 26–27
    filling automatically, **32**, 131
    how to use, 20–22
    naming, 23, **171–174**
    selecting for printing, **54–55**, 168
read-only files, 178
Record command, **78–80**, 151
Record Macro dialog box, **78**, *78*, *151*
records, **88**
    extracting, **95**, 123
    parsing into worksheet columns, 148–149

selecting with Find command, **34**, **94–95**, 121
sorting, **91–92**, 181–182
specifying for deletion, 123
Redo command, **185**
#REF error message, 33
relative cell references, **30**, 81, 114
Relative Record/Absolute Record commands, 81, **153–154**
Relative Record command, 81
Remove Page Break command, **56**, 162
Repeat command, **95**, 174
Replace command/dialog box, **34–35**, *34*, 175
replacing values, labels or formulas, **34–35**, 175
reports, printing, 168
Restore command, **91**
Resume command, **102**, 152
retrieving
    files, 160
    macros sheets, 82
    worksheets, 14–15
Right Align tool, **40**, 134
ROUND function, **19**
Row Height command/dialog box, **46**, *47*, 176, *176*
rows, **5**
    adjusting height of, **46**, *47*, 176
    breaking and printing by, 51
    deleting, **33**, 123
    formatting, 46–47
    hiding or unhiding, **46–47**, 176
    inserting, **32**, 149
Run command, **80**, 152–153
Run Macro dialog box, **80**, *81*

## S

Sampling tools, in Analysis Toolpack Add-in, 109
Save As command, **10–11**, 148, 177, 178–179
Save Workbook command, **178**
saving
    charts, 75–76
    databases, 89
    files as workbooks, 178
    macro sheets, 82
    worksheets, 10–11
Scatter charts. *See* XY (Scatter) charts
Scenario Manager command, 154, **156–157**

scientific notation, 10, 42
scroll bars, navigating with, 6
Search dialog box (Help menu), *146*
searching. *See* finding
security, 178-180
Select Special command/dialog box, **112–114**, *113*
Send to Back/Bring to Front commands, **143**
Series command, **83–84**, *85*, 181
Set Criteria command, **122**
Set Database command, **88**, 122
Set Extract command, **95**, 122
Set Page Break command, *55*, **56**, 162
Set Print Area command, **54–55**, *55*, 168
Set Print Titles command/dialog box, **55–56**, *55*, 168–169
Set Recorder command, **153**
shading of cells, **45–46**, 137
Shift Cells Left button (Edit ➤ Delete command), **124**
Shift Cells Up button (Edit ➤ Delete command), **124**
shortcut keys, for starting macros, 78
Shortcuts menu, advantages of, 27
Show Active Cell command, **181**
Single Step dialog box, **81**
sizing
    charts, 52, 68
    documents, 127
    fonts, 45, 133
    objects, 142
    windows, 125
slide shows, opening, 57
Solver command, **154**
Sort command/dialog box, **91–92**, *92*, 181–182
sorting
    cells or records, **91–92**, 181–182
    databases, 91–92
Sound Note command, 110
spell checking, **35–36**, 182–183
Spelling command, **35–36**, 182–183
Split command, **128**
Stacked column chart tool, 68
starting
    applications, 99
    Excel, 4
    Excel and add-in macros, 109
    Help, 7
    Windows Help application, 147

Start Recorder/Stop Recorder command, **79**, **82**, 152
statistical tools, in Analysis Toolpack Add-in, 109
status bar, **4**, 5
Stop Recorder command, **79**, **82**, 152
Store Macro In options buttons, **79**
Strikeout, selecting, **45**, 133
Style box tool, **139**
Style command, **139**
SUM function, **19**
Surface charts, advantages of, 74
Switch To command, **98**
SYLK files, 58

# T

Tab key, for moving cell selector, 6
Table command, **184**
tables, for what-if analysis, 184
target value modeling, **154–155**
Task List dialog box, **98**, 99, 100
Text box tool (chart toolbar), 68
3D area charts, advantages of, 70
3D area chart tool, 68
3D bar charts, advantages of, 70
3D bar chart tool, 68
3D column charts, advantages of, 70
3D column chart tool, 68
3D line charts, advantages of, 70
3D line chart tool, 68
3D pie chart tool, 68
3D surface chart tool, 68
Tile command, **100**
time-series data comparison, **63**
title bar, **4**, 5
titles. *See also* headers
    designating for printing, **55–56**, 168–169
    placing on charts, 66, 67
toolbar, **4**, 5, 184
Toolbars command, **184**
TrueType fonts, 44, 45
tutorials for Excel, **159**, 190

# U

underlining, selecting, **45**, 133
Undo command, **28**, 185

**199**

◆ Index

Unfreeze Panes command, **128**
Ungroup command, **142**
Unhide command, **126**
unhiding
    columns or rows, **46–47**, 118, 176
    GLOBAL.XLM macro sheet document, 82
    macro sheets, 126
Unprotect Document command, **180**

# V

values, **186**. *See also* formulas; functions
    copying, 28–30
    entering, 9–10
    finding, 34
    formatting, **40–41**, 138
    formatting with AutoFormat, **38–40**, 136
    moving, 31
    repeating with Fill option, 41
    replacing, **34–35**, 175
    seeking with Goal Seek command, 154–156
    and what-if modeling, 156–157
View command, **127**

# W

what-if analysis, with tables, 184
what-if modeling, **156–157**
Window ➤ Arrange command, **125**
Window ➤ Arrange Icons command, **125**
Window ➤ Freeze Panes command, **128**
Window ➤ Hide command, **126**
Window ➤ New Window command, **127**
Window ➤ Split command, **128**
Window ➤ Unfreeze Panes command, **128**
Window ➤ Unhide command, **126**
Window ➤ View command, **127**
Window ➤ Zoom command, **127**
windows, 125, **187**
    for applications, 110–111
    cascading, 100
    opening, 57
    tiling, 100
workbooks, **187**
    opening, 57
    saving files as, 178

worksheets. *See also* cells; columns; formulas; ranges of cells; rows; security
    automatic recalculation of, **17–18**, 112
    compressing into outline form, 160–161
    consolidating and reusing data from, 119
    creating, 7–10
    embedding in documents, 142
    grouping, 144, 187
    linking for mutual updates, **106**, 158
    naming, 11
    navigating, 6
    printing, **50–56**, 166–167
    retrieving, 14–15
    saving, 10–11
    sharing with other applications, 102
    specifying search criteria for, 122
Workspace command, **111**
Wrap Text check box, **135**

# X

.XLA extensions for add-in files, 131
.XLC extensions for charts, 75, 131
.XLM extensions for macro sheets, 79, 131
.XLS extension for databases, 96
.XLS extension for worksheets, 11
.XLS extensions for worksheets and databases, 11, 96, 131
.XLT extensions for template files, 131
.XLW extensions for workbook files, 131, 178
XY (Scatter) charts, advantages of, 74
XY (Scatter) chart tool, 68

# Z

Zoom command/dialog box, **127**, *127*
zoom feature, for previewing pages, **52**, 54

# FREE BROCHURE!

**SYBEX**

Complete this form today, and we'll send you a full-color brochure of Sybex bestsellers.

**Please supply the name of the Sybex book purchased.**

_____

### How would you rate it?

_____ Excellent  _____ Very Good  _____ Average  _____ Poor

### Why did you select this particular book?

_____ Recommended to me by a friend
_____ Recommended to me by store personnel
_____ Saw an advertisement in _____
_____ Author's reputation
_____ Saw in Sybex catalog
_____ Required textbook
_____ Sybex reputation
_____ Read book review in _____
_____ In-store display
_____ Other _____

### Where did you buy it?

_____ Bookstore
_____ Computer Store or Software Store
_____ Catalog (name: _____ )
_____ Direct from Sybex
_____ Other: _____

### Did you buy this book with your personal funds?

_____ Yes  _____ No

### About how many computer books do you buy each year?

_____ 1-3  _____ 3-5  _____ 5-7  _____ 7-9  _____ 10+

### About how many Sybex books do you own?

_____ 1-3  _____ 3-5  _____ 5-7  _____ 7-9  _____ 10+

### Please indicate your level of experience with the software covered in this book:

_____ Beginner  _____ Intermediate  _____ Advanced

### Which types of software packages do you use regularly?

_____ Accounting        _____ Databases          _____ Networks
_____ Amiga             _____ Desktop Publishing _____ Operating Systems
_____ Apple/Mac         _____ File Utilities     _____ Spreadsheets
_____ CAD               _____ Money Management   _____ Word Processing
_____ Communications    _____ Languages          _____ Other _____
                                                           (please specify)

**Which of the following best describes your job title?**

_____ Administrative/Secretarial     _____ President/CEO

_____ Director                                    _____ Manager/Supervisor

_____ Engineer/Technician           _____ Other _____
                                                                                    (please specify)

**Comments on the weaknesses/strengths of this book:** _____

_____

_____

_____

_____

**Name** _____
**Street** _____
**City/State/Zip** _____
**Phone** _____

PLEASE FOLD, SEAL, AND MAIL TO SYBEX

**SYBEX, INC.**
Department M
2021 CHALLENGER DR.
ALAMEDA, CALIFORNIA USA
94501

SYBEX

SEAL

## File
- **New...**
- Open...     Ctrl+F12
- Close
- Links...
- Save     Shift+F12
- Save As...     F12
- Save Workbook...
- Delete...
- Print Preview
- Page Setup...
- Print...     Ctrl+Shift+F12
- Print Report...
- Exit     Alt+F4

## Edit
- Undo Clear     Ctrl+Z
- Repeat Clear
- Cut     Ctrl+X
- Copy     Ctrl+C
- Paste     Ctrl+V
- Clear...     Del
- Paste Special...
- Paste Link
- Delete...
- Insert...
- Insert Object...
- Fill Right     Ctrl+R
- Fill Down     Ctrl+D

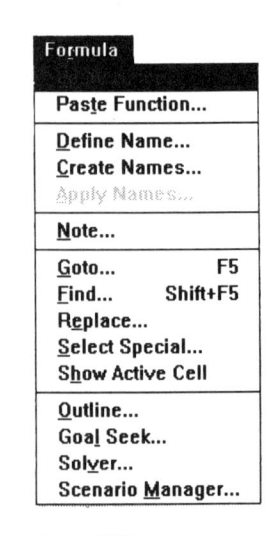

## Formula
- Paste Function...
- Define Name...
- Create Names...
- Apply Names...
- Note...
- Goto...     F5
- Find...     Shift+F5
- Replace...
- Select Special...
- Show Active Cell
- Outline...
- Goal Seek...
- Solver...
- Scenario Manager...

## Format
- Number...
- Alignment...
- Font...
- Border...
- Patterns...
- Cell Protection...
- Style...
- AutoFormat...
- Row Height...
- Column Width...
- Justify
- Bring to Front
- Send to Back
- Group
- Object Properties...

## Data
- Form...
- Find
- Extract...
- Delete
- Set Database
- Set Criteria
- Set Extract
- Sort...
- Series...
- Table...
- Parse...
- Consolidate...
- Crosstab...

## Options
- Set Print Area
- Set Print Titles...
- Set Page Break
- Display...
- Toolbars...
- Color Palette...
- Protect Document...
- Add-ins...
- Calculation...
- Workspace...
- Spelling...
- Group Edit...
- Analysis Tools...

## Macro
- Run...
- Record...
- Start Recorder
- Set Recorder
- Relative Record
- Assign to Object...
- Resume

## Window
- New Window
- Arrange...
- Hide
- Unhide...
- View...
- Split
- Freeze Panes
- Zoom...
- √1 Sheet1

## Help
- Contents     F1
- Search...
- Product Support
- Introducing Microsoft Excel
- Learning Microsoft Excel
- Lotus 1-2-3...
- Multiplan Help...
- About Microsoft Excel...